Dealing with the
S-WORDS

Self-Esteem • Significance • Sex • Secrets • Suicide

Written by
Jason Creech & Sandra Saylor

Publishing

Published by
Innovo Publishing LLC
www.innovopublishing.com
1-888-546-2111

Providing Full-Service Publishing Services for
Christian Authors, Artists & Organizations: Hardbacks, Paperbacks,
eBooks, Audiobooks, Music & Videos

DEALING WITH THE S-WORDS
Copyright © 2011 Innovo Publishing
All rights reserved.

No part of this publication may be reproduced, stored in a retrieval system, or transmitted in any form or by any means electronic, mechanical, photocopying, recording, or otherwise, without the prior written permission of the author.

All scripture quotations, unless otherwise indicated, are taken from the
Holy Bible: New King James Version. Copyright 1982 by Thomas Nelson, Inc.
Used by permission. All rights reserved.

ISBN 13: 978-1-936076-70-3
ISBN 10: 1-936076-70-5

Devotional entries written by Jason Creech
Looking Into the Mirror sections written by Sandra Saylor
Cover design by Jason Creech
Interior Layout by Innovo Publishing

Printed in the United States of America
U.S. Printing History

First Edition: March 2011

Table of Contents

Let's Get Started 5
Self-Esteem 7
Confidence 8
I Double Dog Dare Ya! 10
Identity Crisis 12
Play to Your Strengths 15
To the Moon 17
Thirty-Eight and Still Getting Pimples 19
100,000 RPM 21
When the Lord Is with You 23
Who Do Men Say That I Am? 25
Purpose Precedes Production 28
Success and Significance 30
You Don't Have to Be What You See 31
It Only Takes One to Change the World 34
The Becoming 37
Paying the Price 39
Jesus and the Wrong Crowd 41
Apple Seeds 43
Labels and the Scars They Leave 45
Fighting for Your Destiny 47
No More Talking About It 50
Sex and Secrets 52
Hidden Habits 53
The Third Commandment 55

Coming Out from Among God's People	57
Little Things that Make a Big Difference	60
Peace, Joy, and Rest	63
Porn and Dirty Little Secrets	66
Are You Alone?	68
Dumping Your Date	71
Sex-Esteem	74
He Loves Me . . . He Loves Me Not	76
Somebody's Watching	78
The Esther Challenge	81
Dose of Truth	84
Friends . . . Who Needs 'Em?	88
Suicide	91
A Journey Toward Suicide	92
Failing Faith	94
Heaven or Hell?	96
The Pride of Suicide	98
Make Pain Your Platform	101
What about Samson?	103
Better Safe than Sorry	105
Before You Go	107
Endnotes	108

Let's Get Started

They had just left a wonderful Sunday morning service. My aunt Susie and her family were enjoying a nice lunch with some friends, when their five-year-old son, Dylan, got everyone's attention. In a tone loud enough to silence the entire restaurant, he asked, "Mom, is it okay if I start saying the 's' word?" In her, you're-dead-when-we-get-home voice, she said, "Absolutely not!" He said, "But Mom, I'll say the word holy in front of it!"

This is a book about "S" words. The "Don't go there" words. The topics that get Sunday school teachers replaced and youth pastors fired. Through our time together, I want to address five "s" words:

- Self-esteem
- Significance
- Sex
- Secrets
- Even Suicide

These are topics we all have questions about. For some of us, we've battled with issues revolving around one or more of these words.

Several years ago, I was watching a talk show one afternoon. The host introduced his guest for that day's episode. She was a middle-aged lady with a pitiful story. For the past thirty years, nothing in her life seemed to work out; first there was a terrible childhood followed by sickness, job loss, poverty, foreclosure, and then, an unfaithful husband who left her divorced, broken, and suicidal. It was obvious this highly rated talk show host was about to bless the socks off this poor lady. Before he released his generosity, he asked her this question: "If I could give you anything, what would you want?" I'll never forget her answer. Sitting there crying, she lifted her head out of her hands and said, "Can you give me a new life?"

All the gifts that Hollywood could offer would never be capable of fulfilling her request for a new life.

Allow me to take a minute and explain why this book was written. A few years ago, a public school principal asked me to come to his school and talk to the students about self-esteem. One invitation led to another and soon a team of people joined together and an organization now called Mirror-Mirror was born. Now over 56,000 students have attended one of our events. It's been an incredible ride! To involve the students, we decided to let each school pick one boy and one girl to participate in an extreme makeover. At the beginning of the event, two students are pulled out and taken back stage where our team hooks them up from head to toe. One hour later they come out looking completely different.

Here is one example:

BEFORE

AFTER

From the day Mirror-Mirror began, I've said that we could give these young people everything they wanted on the outside. However, if they don't get some things right on the inside, they will never be the happy, successful people that they were created to be. Happiness is an inside job. Success takes place on the inside first. The tabloids are filled with rich, popular celebrities whose lives are filled with heartache and madness. Rich or poor, popular or unnoticed, we're all looking for the same thing—new life. That's where I hope to lead you. Throughout our time together, we will discover several things God says about life's toughest issues. Thanks for joining me.

Self-Esteem

I have walked down roads of darkness
Secrets buried deep
Shame written all over my face
And before I knew it
I had given myself away
A choice that led me into the darkness
And my voice was lost
My tears choking my throat
Then I caught a glimpse of myself
Used up and tossed away
A silent creature I was
I stood up and shouted
No more do I stay this way
Wash me and cleanse me, Oh God
The silence was broken
And You knew my face
You knew the truth
My choice is now You, my God
I never expected to find You this way
On a long road
But the lies are destroyed here
And I stand not to be given away
For I am given to my Lord
My worth and my hope
Lies here and I find a new day

By Mary Allison

Confidence

I say it all the time: "I could know a thousand and one reasons why I shouldn't do something, but if I'm that one guy who will do anything to fit in, then knowing why I shouldn't do something probably won't keep me from doing it." What we could all use is a dose of confidence. Confidence gives me the ability to stand up, stand out, and be different.

Last year a teenage friend of mine nearly died of a drug overdose. After spending a day together, I asked him what he was going to do. He said, "I'm changing schools." A few weeks later, a young girl I know got into some trouble at school. To solve the problem, she said she wanted to change schools.

To some it may seem like a quick fix. Get away from the negative influences in your school and you won't continue to make dumb choices. But is that true? I don't think the problem is the school or the students in the school. You see, no one can make you get high, get drunk, cut yourself, or anything else for that matter. You make your own choices and so do I. If you didn't have the guts to say no at one school, you'll probably be the same gutless kid at the next school. Your problem is a confidence problem, and you know what? During my first three years of high school, I was the same way.

In my senior year of high school I read something that changed my life. Now I know that we hear that line all the time. I guess I sound like Billy Mayes, the infamous TV salesman with the painted on beard. Trust me—I'm not one of those guys. Jesus Christ radically changed my life. A guy named Phillip gave me a Bible and insisted that I read a chapter each day. Reading wasn't my thing, but he was a lot bigger than me so I did what he said. The more I read, the more my life changed. I went from being a lousy student to making the Dean's List my freshman year of college. I went from being under the peer pressure to being the peer pressure.

You see, God says some incredible things about His people. As His child, I am more than a conqueror through Christ Jesus my Lord. In me dwells the fullness of God's Spirit. He will always lead me into triumph. Nothing can separate me from His love. If God is for me, who can be against me? Because of Christ, I am free from the guilt of sin, blessed, chosen, and filled with power.

God hasn't created us to be failures that merely exist. Before we were ever conceived in our mother's womb, we were conceived in the mind of God. You were created by God and you are loved by Him.

LOOKING INTO THE MIRROR

The Word of God is the only magic book. The dictionary defines magic as "an extraordinary power or influence seemingly from a supernatural force . . . believed to have supernatural power over natural forces." The Word of God has the power to change our lives.

- What is one of your favorite verses? Make a list of two or three of your favorite verses below. Many times, a hint to our life's message is found there.

I Double Dog Dare Ya!

Hebrews 2:18 tells us that Jesus suffered everything that we could possibly suffer, so He could relate to us and aid us in our suffering. I find it hard to believe that the Son of God, who walked on water and did things that Jedi's can only dream of, ever suffered an attack against His confidence. But all through Jesus' life on earth, people were saying, "If You are the Son of God . . . show me a sign or come down from the cross."

The other day I started thinking about the temptation in the wilderness. Satan came to Jesus and said, "If you are the Son of God, command these stones to become bread." Now, hold up! The Bible calls that a temptation. What kind of temptation is that? Furthermore, what's wrong with turning stones into bread? The law doesn't prohibit it. The commandments don't forbid it. What's the big deal? I'll tell you one thing, if I were the Son of God, and my archenemy challenged me to do something harmless like that, I would have snapped my fingers and *BAM!*—bread would have covered that wilderness.

>   White bread
>   Wheat bread
>   French bread
>   Corn bread
>   Cheesy bread
>   Bread sticks
>   Garlic bread
>   Homemade bread
>   Store-bought bread
>   Frozen bread

>   You get the picture.

The unbelievable thing to me is that Jesus didn't try to prove anything. You see, when you're confident, you don't have to prove yourself to anyone. People who respond to a challenge are weak people. At times, these people might appear to be all big and bad, but mark it down, they are full of insecurities. Every day they feel they must prove something to someone. Listen, if you are one of those people, do yourself a favor and bury yourself in God's Word. Through its pages you will find confidence and freedom.

LOOKING INTO THE MIRROR

Jesus' only weapon against the devil in the wilderness was the Word of God.

- Are you in a wilderness experience? If so, what is it?

- What words are you using as weapons?

Identity Crisis

If you've been in one of our school assemblies, you've probably heard the stats. In 2006, 1.2 million Ford trucks were sold in the United States. At the close of 2006, 4.1 million Americans had subscribed to XM Radio. During that same year, 10.2 million Americans received plastic surgery. For every one person who bought a new Ford truck, ten people bought a new face, a new tummy, or a new tush.

We have a sick obsession with looking picture perfect. Most young ladies want to look like the girl on the magazine cover. Most young men want to look like the guy on the big screen. For many of us, this obsession is deadly. In America, teen suicide outnumbers teen homicide three to two. In other cultures, people commit suicide because they believe they have found something worth dying for. In our culture, we often commit suicide because we've yet to find something worth living for.

We obtain yet complain more than any other society in the world. Let me be the first, or maybe just the next, to say, "Happiness is not in Hollywood!" You can have it all and still be empty. Have you ever received something you always wanted and a few days later the newness wore off and life was a bore again? I have.

The Bible says something about our identity that you must know. God said, "Let us make man in our image." We were created to reflect God's image, His nature, His goodness, His character, His talents, His creativity, and His power. As guys, for some reason, we grow up thinking that the more beer we drink, the more guys we whip, and the more women we chase, the more of a man we are. These guys are the provers—always trying to prove their manhood. But a real man reflects God's image. The more like God I am, the more of a man I am. A fish isn't content hanging off a plaque over someone's mantle. That's not its intended purpose. As people were created to reflect God's image, we will never be truly satisfied until we are doing what we were born to do.

The first major identity crisis appeared in the Garden of Eden. God created mankind to mirror His image. However, when Adam and Eve (the first man and woman) sinned, they ceased to do what they were created to do. At that moment, a major identity crisis occurred. Sin introduced humanity to guilt, regret, depression, anxiety, fear, torment, and isolation.

In junior high biology, we learn that half of our chromosomes come from our father and the other half come from our mother. Believe it or not, our parents are in us! That's kind of depressing isn't it?

You see, because Adam and Eve sinned, sin became a part of our genetic makeup. Our problem with sin occurred before we ever committed our first sin—we were born sinners. Sin was in us at conception. That's why Jesus had to be born of a virgin. It is true that He was 100 percent man, and 100 percent God. Half of His chromosomes came from humanity—Mary, and half of His chromosomes came from divinity—God. The blood that ran through the body of Jesus was unlike any blood of any man who has ever lived.

It's important we realize that our problem with sin is much bigger than our bad habits. It's more complicated than that. Jesus didn't die on a cross just to keep you from saying four-letter words and cheating on your history test. Jesus died on the cross to snatch the sin out of your DNA. The cross is about a blood transfusion. Christianity is about a relationship with Jesus Christ that sets us free from sin! That's why 2 Corinthians 5:17 says, "If any man be in Christ, he is a new creation, old things have passed away; behold, all things become new."

As good as life can be at times, mark this down, you will never be fulfilled until you do what you were created to do—reflect God's image. Embrace God's love and mercy. Receive the forgiveness brought by the cross, and begin to do what you were created to do—reflect!

LOOKING INTO THE MIRROR

- Make a list of all the things that you would like to change about you.

- In the scope of eternity, how many of those things really matter? Mark a line through the ones that don't.

- What things do matter in light of eternity?

- What are some unhealthy consequences of a picture-perfect obsession?

Play to Your Strengths

As a child I had terrible self-esteem. I started wearing glasses in the third grade, and out of all the frames I could have chosen, my mother picked out the dorkiest pair. I felt like a big Freak-Boy! The one group of kids who always seemed to be on top of the world was athletes. I dreamed of being the coolest kid in the school, running touchdowns, breaking backboards, and taking a bow at the end of every game. The problem is I'm not athletic. But I didn't let that technicality stop me.

First, it was pee-wee football. I was the kid who picked up the ball and ran into the wrong end zone. The good thing about pee-wee football is everyone gets to play. If you stink, you probably don't know you do. Then came Little-League baseball. Three years of riding the bench and I was fed up. Junior-high football came and went with no great stories to tell. I was so bad that my jersey didn't match all the other players on my team. Basketball was certainly not for me, and one night in karate class, I broke my hand trying to break a board.

In high school, I wanted to have my own letterman jacket; so I signed up for football. On the first day of practice, the coach asked me to run a pass play. He took out one of our best players and put me in his place. Now this guy was good at everything. Have you ever known someone like that? If it required a ball and coordination, he could do it.

The ball was snapped. I ran about ten yards, cut across the field, and the quarterback threw the ball. I have no idea where that hole came from! Some groundhog must have dug that baby just for me. About the time the ball reached my hands, I fell in. I almost broke my ankle, and I busted my face on the practice field. Who has big holes in their practice field anyway?

Now, think about this: I was trying to build my self-esteem by doing something that I was not naturally gifted to do. I wasn't playing to my strengths. On the flip side, I'm a great artist. When I was a kid, I won every art show coming and going; but I didn't think artists were as cool as athletes. Don't waste your time trying to be something that you were not created to be. Has anyone ever told you, "You can be anything you want to be?" I don't think so! It doesn't work that way. But, we can be what we were created to be.

Concentrate on the areas you naturally excel in and focus your energy there. If you weren't born to be a nuclear physicist, that's okay. Just remember to play to your strengths.

LOOKING INTO THE MIRROR

Author Laurie Beth Jones says that many gifts come naturally to us, so we usually don't recognize them as gifts.

- Name five things you enjoy doing. Maybe those are gifts.

To the Moon

If I were to ask you, "What makes you unique?" what would you say? I'm amazed at how short the lists are when I ask young people that question. I've often had people say nothing at all. In one of our news interviews, one young lady said, "I'm ugly, I hate myself, and I suck at everything I do."

Everything about you is uniquely designed.
Everything about you is one of a kind.

Several decades ago, biologists discovered that everyone has a unique DNA code. This discovery revolutionized police investigations. Science tells us that our bodies contain 100 trillion strands of DNA.[1] Each strand of DNA is six feet long. Your body contains 600 trillion feet of DNA information. Let me put this in perspective for you. The moon is 340,649,205 feet from the earth. If you could drive to the moon traveling 70 m.p.h., never slowing down or stopping, it would take 135 days to make a one-way trip. Imagine the gas bill! Now think about this . . . your DNA, your 600 trillion feet of DNA information, would travel to the moon and back—8,806 times. You are special in 600 trillion ways!

A few years ago, I bought a Corvette. I love old muscle cars and I've always been a Corvette fan. I bought a repair manual at a local parts store. This repair manual told me everything I needed to know about a Corvette from the years 1968–1982. Every part and its function were listed in the pages of the manual. By using the manual, I could completely disassemble and reassemble my Corvette. The book was only 289 pages thick.

When scientists mapped the 3 billion codes of one human set of genes, the project filled 75,490 pages.[2] And that's only the explanation of our personal set of genes. Nowhere in those pages will you find out how your eyes work, or how your ears hear. Do you see how uniquely and intricately you were created?

No two people have the same DNA. No two people have the same genes. No one has your hair, your eyes, your smile, your talents, or your gifts. You are wonderfully made! It's so important that you realize you are the way you are because of why you are. You don't build hospitals and McDonalds the same way. One building's purpose is completely different than the other. You are uniquely gifted and handcrafted for your purpose.

In Psalm 139:14–16, David wrote, "I will praise You, for I am fearfully and wonderfully made; marvelous are Your works, and that my soul knows very well. My frame was not hidden from You, when I was made in secret, and skillfully wrought in the lowest parts of the earth. Your eyes saw my substance, being yet unformed, and in Your book they all were written . . ." Apparently, God has a book much bigger than my Corvette repair manual. In this book, all our parts are listed. You weren't thrown together. You are the work of a skillful artist and great is the work of His hands!

LOOKING INTO THE MIRROR

David says in Psalm 139:7-8, "I can never escape from your spirit! I can never get away from your presence! If I go up to heaven, you are there; if I make my bed in hell, you are there."

- Can you think of a dark place in your life where you may have felt like His presence was not there?

- Looking back on that experience, what might have God been teaching you or doing in you during that time?

Thirty-Eight and Still Getting Pimples

We live in a society that says the more attractive you are the more confident you'll be. Many studies have been conducted to support this idea. I'm all for dressing for success, taking care of our bodies, eating right, and exercising. All that is great, but I do have a problem with the philosophy. If being beautiful, sexy, and attractive makes you happy, what happened to celebrities like Elvis Presley, Marilyn Monroe, Anna Nicole Smith, and a multitude of others?

I'm thirty-eight years old and I still get pimples. If day-to-day success is dependent upon my clear complexion, then I'm in bad shape. So many people think they would be happier if they could change this, remove that, add a little over here, and take some off there.

The Bible tells a story of two sisters who both loved the same man. Actually, they were both married to the same man. Now, being from Kentucky, I've seen some weird stuff but that ranks up there pretty high.

The sisters were Rachel and Leah. Their husband's name was Jacob. Jacob was crazy about Rachel from the moment he first laid eyes on her. His marriage to Leah was a mistake—literally. Jacob was supposed to marry Rachel but their dad, Laban, switched the bride. The next morning Jacob woke up beside the wrong girl.

Genesis, Chapter 29, says that Leah was "tender eyed." Other versions say her eyes were delicate or weak. Some say that the phrase "tender eyed" implies that she was unattractive or unpleasant to look at. I like the New Living Translation's twist on it. It says, "There was no sparkle in Leah's eyes." Perhaps she bore the look of rejection. Have you ever seen brokenness in someone's eyes? Maybe that was Leah. One thing was for sure . . . she was miserable.

Rachel was barren and unable to give Jacob a child. The first time Leah got pregnant she named their son Reuben, which means affliction. She said, "The Lord has surely looked on my affliction. Now therefore, my husband will love me." Several more times she conceived and bore Jacob sons. With each pregnancy she would say, "Now this time Jacob will be attached to me. Because of this child, he will love me." But something happened between the third and fourth child. The first three boys were named after their mother's anguish.

Simeon means unloved and Levi means attached. Then came boy number four. She named him Judah, which means praise. Leah declared, "Now I will praise the Lord."

No longer would Leah allow herself to be shaped by the rejection of Jacob. No longer would she compare herself to her sister Rachel. She no longer felt the need to "win the approval of anyone." Leah had encountered God. She had met the Lord. Rejection gave way to God's unfailing love. All she could do was shout with uncontrollable praise. The end of Genesis 29:35 says, "Then she stopped bearing." For years, Leah had been crawling in the bed with someone hoping to find love. With each sexual encounter, she felt more and more alone. Finally, she said, "That's enough!" Then she stopped bearing children. In other words, she stopped allowing Jacob to use her. She didn't need his love; she had God's.

LOOKING INTO THE MIRROR

God gives consolation prizes. Many times on TV game shows, when contestants do not win the big prize, they are given a consolation prize for "not winning." But with God, His consolation prizes are better than the big prize. Leah was hoping for the prize of Jacob's love, but she did not get it. However, she got the prize of many sons, which in her day was the crème de la crème!

The last child she bore was named Dinah, which means "justice." And when Jacob was dying, he asked to be buried beside Leah. She also ended up being Jesus' great-great-great- . . . great-grandma!

- Think about something that you really wanted but didn't get. Now, step back and take a look at your life. Do you see any consolation prizes?

- Spend the next few days asking the Lord to show you some of your consolation prizes. Even dare to ask Him for more—double for your trouble! See Zechariah 9:12.

100,000 RPM

I don't think it's possible with words to express how remarkable and complex life is. Take for example bacterial flagellum. The flagellum is an ion-powered rotary motor, anchored in the membranes surrounding the bacterial cell.[3] In 1973, it was discovered that some bacteria swim by rotating their flagella. This tiny flagellum is about 1/20,000 of an inch in size. Because of its complexity, many scientists refer to bacterial flagellum as the evolutionists' nightmare. Notice the illustration below:

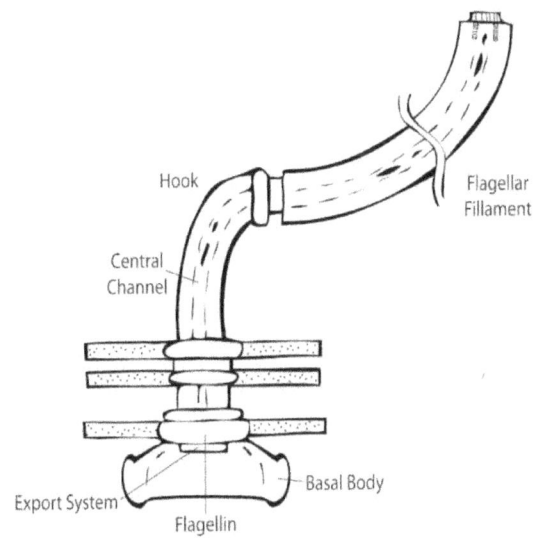

To put this into proper perspective let's compare the flagellum to a rail car. Rail cars are those long, skinny drag racers with fat rear tires and monster motors. Rail cars have an incredible amount of horse power. When a rail car launches, it moves from 0 to 345 m.p.h. in only 4.5 seconds. One racing commentator said that if a new Z06 Corvette raced by a rail car at 200 m.p.h., and the rail car launched the moment the Vette passed, in a quarter mile, the rail car would beat the Vette and shatter its windows as it raced by. One racer told me that a common injury among rail car racers is retina separation. When a racer releases his parachute, the negative G-force causes the retina to separate from the driver's pupil. This is one awesome machine.

Now the crazy thing is that the engine of a rail car only turns at less than 8,000 r.p.m. The motor actually melts down within the first eighth of a mile and pushes its way through the last half. At the end of the run, the motor is junk. However, the flagellum's tiny rotary motor turns at 10,000 r.p.m. It can stop spinning within a quarter turn and instantly start spinning the other direction at exactly the same rate of speed. Howard Berg of Harvard University called it, "The most efficient motor in the universe." However, the meanest motors man can create are no match for the intelligence of God's creation. How awesome it is when we realize the thought and planning that God invested in creating us.

LOOKING INTO THE MIRROR

- We all have the ability to create. We create with our words. If all your words are prayers and if all your prayers are answered, what will your world look like?

When the Lord Is with You

A wise old man once said, "When you know the good Lord is with you, you're the most powerful person in the room."

A few weeks ago I came across an interesting passage that revolves around two kings. Well, one was a king and the other would soon be. King Saul was the first king of Israel. In the beginning he was humble, handsome, a fine warrior, and for a season, the Lord was with him, or should I say, "He was with the Lord." In time, Saul became less concerned with what the Lord thought about him, and more concerned with what everyone around him thought about him. The applause of the people cost him the presence of the Lord.

David was a young man of no great importance. He made his living tending his father's sheep. He was the youngest, the baby, and the least of all his brothers. Now these two men were of no real comparison; however, look at the following verse: "Now Saul was afraid of David, because the Lord was with him . . ." (1 Samuel 18:12).

Saul was a king. David was a shepherd and a part-time musician. Saul led the armies of Israel. David followed his daddy's sheep. Saul was a giant compared to David. When going before Goliath, David tried to put on Saul's armor but it was so big on him that he could hardly move. There was no reason for Saul to fear David.

Saul was bigger.

Saul was broader.

Saul carried a sword.

David carried a staff.

Saul carried a shield.

David carried a harp.

But . . . the Lord was with David.

And that scared the king.

If you're a follower of Christ, there's more to you than meets the eye. If you're a follower of Christ, then the Lord is with you. The armies of hell shake in the presence of God's children. Why? Because where we are, God is! He's in us and we're in Him. Colossians 1:26–27 says, "The mystery which has been hidden from ages and from generations, but now has been revealed to His saints. To them God willed to make known what are the riches of the glory of this mystery among the Gentiles: which is Christ in you, the hope of glory." Once again, we see this same thought in 1 John 4:4: "You are of God, little children, and have overcome them, because He who is in you is greater than he who is in the world." Notice Colossians 3:2–3, "Set your mind on things above, not on things on the earth. For you died, and your life is hidden with Christ in God." As a follower of Christ, He is in me and I am in Him. Truly there is only one thing that matters in life, and that is that the Lord is with us.

LOOKING INTO THE MIRROR

- Think of a time when you know that the Lord was with you. What happened?

- How does knowing that God is with you affect your confidence?

Who Do Men Say That I Am?

Shortly after I created a Facebook account, I discovered the notification box on the lower right side of the computer monitor. When I clicked on the box, I was surprised to see that several of my so-called friends had answered some questions about me in a survey. Of course I clicked to see what had been said. I glanced over questions like: "Would Jason bail you out of jail? Could you trust him with a secret?" Those kinds of questions. Each question was answered to my liking. But one question at the bottom of the survey caught my eye . . .

"Do you think Jason is cute?"

Seven "friends" answered that question, and all seven of my blind and stupid "friends" said no. This confirmed all my suspicions. I knew that my mid-thirties had not been good to me, but these seven wonderful people gutted me. I ran to my wife and pouted. She kissed me on the forehead and told me I would always be cute in her eyes. Thanks, dear! I thought about calling my mom, but I wasn't that desperate. To the basement I went. That's where my office is. On my desk I have an old wedding picture of Melissa and me. As I looked at that picture, I started asking myself, "Why are you so concerned about what people think about you?" I know it's not healthy, but from time to time I still want to know what everyone else thinks. Sitting in my basement office I started thinking about Hebrews 2:18. It's one of my favorite verses in the Bible. I want to show you this verse from a variety of translations.

"For in that He Himself has suffered, being tempted, He is able to aid those who are tempted."
New King James

"Since He Himself has gone through suffering and testing, He is able to help us when we are being tested."
New Living Translation

"For since He Himself has now been through suffering and temptation, He knows what it is like when we suffer and are tempted, and He is wonderfully able to help us."
The Book Translation

"And now that Jesus has suffered and was tempted, he can help anyone else who is tempted."
Contemporary English Version

This verse comforts me for the obvious reason; whatever I go through in life, Jesus faced it and conquered it. He then can relate to my suffering like no one else can. When I'm tempted, He can assist me like no other. But how could Jesus relate to me and my Facebook friends? Did Jesus have a Facebook? We know He didn't, but He did have to deal with the negative things people said about Him.

In Matthew 16:13 Jesus asked His disciples, "Who do men say that I, the Son of Man, am?" His disciples replied, "Some say John the Baptist, some Elijah, and others Jeremiah or one of the prophets." Jesus was the Son of God, not just another prophet! But many simply did not believe. Despite the miraculous birth, the star in the east, the fulfillment of prophecies, the miracles, the crowds, the amazing teachings, still many did not believe. Finally one night Jesus asked some of those closest to Him, "Guys, what are they saying about Me? When I'm not around, what's their opinion? What's the buzz on the streets? Who do men say that I am?"

Jesus knows what it's like to face criticism, but He knew who He was. No matter what they thought, He knew He was the Son of the Living God, the Savior of the world, the Lamb of God, the First and the Last, the Redeemer of all that was lost, and that was all that mattered. Know who you are! Know who God says that you are!

That's all that matters.

LOOKING INTO THE MIRROR

- Who are you? I'm not asking for your name. Go deeper than that. Who are you right now?

- Who do you believe God created you to be?

- An early twentieth-century Scottish preacher, by the name of Oswald Chambers, said in his devotional, *My Utmost for His Highest*, that we are responsible for the depth of our character but God is responsible for the breadth of our ministry. What do you think this means?

Purpose Precedes Production

Miles Munroe is one of my favorite authors. In his book, *Pursuit of Purpose*, he says, "Purpose always precedes production." Nothing is made without a purpose. Everything created has an intended purpose. Think about a bulldozer. A few guys didn't weld together a bunch of metal, paint it yellow, stand back and say, "What are we gonna do with that?" That's not how it happened. Someone got tired of calloused hands and throbbing back pain and said, "There's got to be a better way to do this!" First, there was a purpose, then came the product, and the product was made perfect for its purpose.

Long before you became a reality, God thought you up. God looked down from heaven and saw a need in this world during this time and His response to that need was "you." Every day you wake up is a testimony that today the world needs you. You were fashioned for a purpose and you were created perfect for your purpose. Your gifts, talents, passions, and abilities all point to your divine purpose. God wired you up for success. He spent much time planning and thinking before He began putting you together. Draftsmen make about 27,000 drawings for the manufacturing of a new car. God did more than that before He made you.

In the book of Exodus, the children of Israel were living as slaves in Egypt. Their cry for freedom was heard by God and God responded by visiting Moses. Israel needed a leader and Moses was the perfect man for the job. Actually, Moses was the only man created for the job. Moses, like the rest of us, was created to make an impact in the world that no one else could make.

Four times God said to Moses, "Go to Egypt and tell Pharaoh to let My people go. Then, lead the people out of slavery to the land that I will give to them and their children." Over and over again Moses said, "No God, I can't do it. I'm not your guy. I don't have what it takes to pull it off. Sorry, I can't do it!" Moses finally asked God to find someone else. At that point, the Bible says, "The anger of the Lord blazed hot against Moses." Why was God angry? Because there was no one else to find. God had no plan B. God had plan A and

Moses was plan A. Furthermore, the created can't tell the creator what He can and cannot do. God will never ask you to do something that you're not capable of doing. The next time God puts an idea in your heart, be confident that it is do-able.

LOOKING INTO THE MIRROR

We learn in Exodus 4:10 that Moses had a speech problem.

- What excuses have you made for not succeeding?

- See Exodus 4:11 to see God's reply to excuses.

Success and Significance

You brought me up from the pit.
Out of the clay, You pulled me and set me on the wheel.
You're shaping this vessel as it seems good to the potter to form.
For who am I to say, "Who are You to still find fault in me?"
Who am I to question the way that I am?
For the potter has power over the clay.
I am Your spokesman
formed out of the clay that You now pour Your oil into.
I've been placed in the oven to be tried,
to be perfected as pure gold.
For my God is a consuming fire.

By Jamie Jones

You Don't Have to Be What You See

Unfortunately, 95 percent of what we see on TV involves celebrities who fail to be role models. Many of America's parents are still living like teenagers, while their children pay the consequences. While we've been busy building a nation, we've lost a generation.

I travel weekly and talk to thousands of teenagers. It's not uncommon for me to sit in a guidance counselor's office with a troubled student who needs to pour his or her heart out to someone. I've listened to young ladies weep bitterly after being raped by an older family member. I've met with students the day after their siblings committed suicide. I recently met a boy whose daddy traded him for a video game. After one young man's father passed away, he discovered that the man wasn't actually his father. The man had purchased him from his mother at a truck stop not long after he was born. Some of the stories are too difficult to imagine and hardly believable. I'm often reminded of a verse in the third chapter of Joel: "They have cast lots for My people, have given a boy as payment for a harlot, and sold a girl for wine, that they may drink" (Joel 3:3).

In our school assemblies I always tell students, "You don't have to be what you see!" For many kids today, all they see is drugs, alcohol, violence, and one sexual affair after the other. In most cases, we become what we behold. However, through Christ, we have the ability to break the cycle. We can't do much about where we've come from, but we can control where we're going. We choose whether we live as victims or victors. The choice is ours.

For all the parents who are still living like you're a college freshman—grow up! Don't expect anyone else to fix what you've spent your entire life messing up. Wake up! Call on God! As long as there's breath in your body, there's hope. No one will ever impact your child as much as you.

The notorious Al (Scarface) Capone had a lawyer nicknamed Easy Eddie. Eddie was very good at what he did and his skill at maneuvering around in the courtroom kept Big Al out of jail for a long time. As a result, Capone made sure that Eddie was "treated right." For instance, Eddie's family occupied a fenced-in mansion that filled an entire Chicago city block. Eddie lived the mobster's high-life and seemed to show no consideration for the atrocities that went on around him. However, Eddie did have a tender spot. He had a son who he loved more than life itself. He worried about the legacy that he was leaving his young boy. Despite all his wealth, he could never leave his boy a good name; and that tormented him. One day, Easy Eddie made a difficult decision. To somehow right the wrong he had done, he decided to testify against Capone and the mob. Within a year, he was gunned down on a lonely Chicago street.

Years later, Eddie's son enlisted in the armed forces. The Second World War produced many heroes. One such man was Lieutenant Commander Butch O'Hare. O'Hare was a fighter pilot. One day his squadron was sent on a mission. Shortly after leaving the aircraft carrier, he realized that someone had forgotten to top off his fuel tank. Knowing he would not have enough fuel to complete his mission, he dropped out of formation and made his way back to the ship.

On his way back, he noticed a squadron of Japanese planes that were speeding toward the American fleet. With the American fighters gone, the ship was defenseless. There was no time to lose. O'Hare flew directly into the Japanese formation. His wing-mounted .50-caliber guns blazed as he charged in. Weaving in and out, he tried to gun down or clip as many enemy aircrafts as possible. Finally, the Japanese pilots flew away.

The film from his gun-camera told it all. He had, in fact, knocked off five enemy aircrafts and saved his crew aboard the carrier. The Chicago O'Hare airport is named after Lieutenant Commander Butch O'Hare. He was Easy Eddie's son.

Despite the mistakes of our past, it's never too late to do the right thing!

LOOKING INTO THE MIRROR

We've all made mistakes.

- Think about some you've made that you don't want to repeat again. How can you avoid doing the same thing again?

- What have you learned from the mistakes of your past?

- What do you want to be remembered for?

It Only Takes One to Change the World

My wife and I grew up in southeastern Kentucky. There's nothing like the beautiful mountains in the fall and the spring hikes in the woods. At one time, this land boomed with growth. The rich coal inside these Kentucky mountains brought lots of industry to the Appalachian area. Today, most of these coal towns look more like ghost towns. Many of the folks left behind find it hard to be optimistic. Many critical spirits have killed the dreams of future generations. I often tell young people not to believe everything they hear.

In John Maxwell's book, *Attitude 101*, he tells the following story: "During the first half of the twentieth century, many sports experts believed that no runner could run a mile in less than four minutes. And for a long time, they were right. But then, on May 6, 1954, British runner and university student, Roger Bannister, ran a mile in 3 minutes 59.4 seconds during a meet in Oxford. Less than two months later, another runner, Australian, John Landy, also broke the four-minute barrier. Later, dozens and then hundreds of others broke it."

Now why is this? Why is it that for centuries no one does what the experts say is impossible, but the moment someone does, hundreds do? I'll tell you why. Everyone is looking for someone to defy the odds, someone who will dare to do the impossible, and someone who refuses to live his or her life based on the expectations of those around them. When someone like that arises, everyone follows. Everyone is looking for someone to lead the way.

In the seventeenth chapter of 1 Samuel, we have a story that finds its way into every children's Bible—the story of David and Goliath. Goliath was a champion of the Philistine army. The Philistines had camped on one mountain top and across the valley. King Saul and his men set up camp on another mountain top. Before the battle began, the Philistines made a challenge. Instead of the two armies meeting in the valley, each side would choose a champion to fight to the death. If King Saul's man won, the Philistines would become the servants of Israel. On the other hand, if Goliath won, King Saul and his men would be the slaves of their enemies.

Now on one hand, this sounds great. Instead of thousands of men dying, only one man has to die. But the problem was Goliath. He was 9'9" tall. In front of him was a man carrying a shield. His breastplate weighed 125 pounds. Try fighting someone with 125 pounds hanging off your shoulders! This guy was gigantic! No one would fight Goliath. Day after day, Goliath would come down the valley and challenge someone to come and fight. Now, the Bible describes King Saul as standing head and shoulders above all the men of Israel, but not even the king would go out to fight. Everyone believed that no one could beat the Philistine champion.

Then David arrived on the scene. He was the youngest of his brothers and he was not a soldier. He was a shepherd. David volunteered to fight Goliath. Of course, everyone had something ugly to say about that. They weren't too keen on being slaves. Now, you probably know the outcome of the story. David killed Goliath; but, my favorite part of the story begins at verse 52. After David killed the giant, the next verse says, "And the men of Israel and of Judah arose, and shouted, and pursued the Philistines . . ."

Now wait a doggone minute! These same boys were scared to death a few verses earlier. What happened?

- Someone did the impossible.
- Someone did what everyone said could not be done.
- Someone paved the way.
- Someone dared to live beyond the expectations of those around them.

Someone once said that a critic is a legless man who tries to teach everyone else how to run. In John Mason's book, *An Enemy Called Average*, he writes, "Shoot for the moon, even if you miss you'll still land among the stars." Remember, it only takes one to lead the way.

LOOKING INTO THE MIRROR

David's training for the extraordinary Goliath victory came in a lonely ordinary field, keeping his dad's sheep—I Samuel 17:32–37. You can't have the extraordinary without the ordinary.

- What ordinary field are you training in right now?

- What might God be training you for?

The Becoming

Every little kid has a dream of being someone incredible. Whether it's an astronaut, rock star, pro athlete, or if you're like my son, you dream of being Spiderman. The point is, everyone has a dream of greatness. However, dreams never determine what we become. What we become is based upon the daily decisions we make. The question is not, "What do you want to be?" The question is, "What are you becoming?"

Some time back, I was with a young man who was busted for using drugs. He had the typical teenage attitude and he listened to no one. When I talked with him last, he was still getting high. I asked him what he wanted to do when he graduated high school. His dream was to be an architect. Now, that's a great dream, so I asked him, "Why was I sent here to talk to you today?"

"Because I've been doing drugs and getting in trouble at school," he said.

I said, "Bro, let me share something with you. You are not becoming an architect. You're becoming a loser! You may dream of being an architect, but dreams never determine who you become. Our decisions determine who we become. Decisions determine destiny—we will become what we are becoming."

When I was a little boy, my dad used to always push me to do my best in school. He would say that my fifth-grade report card would affect me for the rest of my life. To a fifth-grade boy the "rest of my life" seemed hard to comprehend. I now realize that he was trying to teach me the importance of today. Our today is what shapes our tomorrow. It's amazing to me how so many young people surround themselves with bad company and develop bad habits; yet for some reason, they don't realize the long-term effect of their choices.

A friend of mine, Jay Haizlip, always says, "No one was born to be a loser. If you get to the end of your life, and realize that you're nothing but a loser, you can't blame anyone but you. You can't blame your parents. You can't blame your school. You can't blame God or the preacher across the street. You can't blame the system. You can't blame anyone but you."

When my brother was younger, someone asked him these two questions:

1. What do you dream of doing someday?
2. What are you doing today that's getting you one step closer to that dream?

So, if your tomorrow is shaped by your today, what is your tomorrow looking like? What kind of future are you creating for yourself? Remember, yesterday is in the past, tomorrow isn't promised, all we have is today. What are you becoming today?

LOOKING INTO THE MIRROR

- What is your greatest dream?

- Make two lists: one that lists what you need to stop doing to achieve the dream, and on the other, list what you need to start doing to achieve your dream.

Paying the Price

When God wants to propel you toward your destiny, He will always surround you with the right kind of people. When the devil wants to keep you from your destiny, he will always surround you with the wrong kind of people. Either way, the people around us will be a catapult or a casket for our destinies. If you want to achieve anything in life, you must surround yourself with the right kind of people.

From the day I became a follower of Jesus, I have given myself to the dream of seeing a young generation rise up in America and become the people God created them to be. Now, I'm a big dreamer. But growing up in an impoverished area meant resources and opportunities were few and far between. The culture of that region was very critical of ambition and innovation. For example, according to the U.S. Census Bureau, 25 percent of folks living in that county of Southeastern Kentucky who are twenty-five years old or older have less than a ninth-grade education. Only 11 percent have some college experience. A recent study conducted by Reach of Louisville revealed that 28 percent of the children living in southeastern Kentucky do not have working parents, and 42 percent of the children living in that area of the state live below the poverty level.

Shortly after my wife and I were married, we moved to Alabama and then on to Atlanta, Georgia. While living in Atlanta, I heard about a youth pastor who had grown one of America's largest local church youth ministries. Turned out, he had relocated to the Atlanta area and was working out of a church about forty minutes away from our apartment. I started visiting his youth services, robbing ideas, and loving every minute of it. After a few weeks, I introduced myself to him and asked if I could take him to lunch. He directed me to his secretary and she redirected me a time or two and nothing ever became of it.

But I am relentless. I wouldn't take no for an answer! We finally got a date but it was rescheduled and later canceled. It wasn't long after that when our home in Alabama started falling apart—no joke! A contractor discovered asbestos, the roof starting leaking in two or three places, and the air conditioning unit stopped working. I couldn't rent it and I couldn't sell it. There we were, trying to be obedient to God and chase after the dream He had put in our hearts, and all we were getting was dumped on. Now wouldn't you know it, during those circumstances, this youth pastor's secretary called me up and asked me if I would still be willing to take him to lunch? Before I could get a word out, she told me that he would be bringing someone from his staff also. Now, I would have to feed three people and they named the restaurant.

My wife, Melissa, asked me what I was going to do and where I would get the extra money. I took my one-carat diamond college class ring to a pawn shop and got a $100 out of it. The lady took it in the back to look it over. She came back out and said, "This ring is worth much more than the $100, but that's all that I can give you." I took the money and treated my new friends to lunch. Six months later, the youth pastor offered me a job.

If you want to be great at something, pay the price to get around the right kind of people. Shadow the best and never settle for less. Jesus said that a servant is not above his master or a student above his teacher. In other words, you will never rise above those you follow. We should always strive to glean from the best, serve them, wash their car, or carry their briefcase. The benefits are priceless.

LOOKING INTO THE MIRROR

Elisha wanted to be like Elijah. At one point, Elijah tried to discourage Elisha from following him but Elisha kept pursuing. When Elijah went to heaven in a chariot, his mantle dropped on Elisha (2 Kings 2).

- Who are you following?

- If you become what you follow, then what are you becoming?

Jesus and the Wrong Crowd

As the ministry of Jesus grew in fame, several so-called friends tried to talk some sense into Him. Notice the verse below:

"And the multitude cometh together again, so that they could not so much as eat bread. And when His friends heard of it, they went out to lay hold on Him: for they said, 'He is beside Himself'" (Mark 3:20-21).

Now let me paint a clear picture of what was going on. Jesus started healing people, cleansing lepers, casting demons out of folks, and thousands began following Him. The more He began doing what He was born to do, the more hell sent people to belittle Him. At some point in our lives, someone around us will try to keep us from being who we are destined to be. We see here that even Jesus had a few folks in His circle of friends who tried to keep Him from being who the Heavenly Father wanted Him to be.

We see a similar story in Mark chapter 5 beginning in verse 21. A man, whose daughter was on her death bed, found Jesus and asked Him to come heal her. As they were walking, a very ill lady broke through the crowd and grabbed Jesus by His garment. While He paused to talk with the lady, someone came from the father's house and said, "It's too late. Your daughter just passed away." Jesus encouraged the father to believe. At that point, Jesus refused to let anyone follow Him except Peter, James, and John. When they arrived at the man's home, they were met by a host of mourners. Now look at verses 39–40:

"When He came in, He said to them 'Why make this commotion and weep? The child is not dead, but sleeping.' And they ridiculed Him. But when He had put them all outside, He took the father and the mother of the child, and those who were with Him, and entered where the child was lying."

The closer Jesus got to releasing this miracle, the more He separated Himself from the doubters. Remember: when you start to do what you were created to do, you have to be careful who you have around you. Someone once said that success can be summed up in four, short stages:

1. They don't believe in you.
2. They make fun of you.
3. They put your name in all their jokes.
4. They stand in line for your autograph.

Surround yourself with the right kind of people!

LOOKING INTO THE MIRROR

- Have you ever had someone constantly belittle you? What did he say?

- What was your response?

- When people like that pop up in your life, what's the best way to deal with them?

- How can you keep their words from damaging your potential?

Apple Seeds

Reva Kasey is one of my mom's old high-school friends who turned out to be about as radical as John the Baptist. She is a fiery redhead with a passion for young people and enough guts to charge hell with a water pistol. I'll never forget something she said one day: "Anyone can tell you how many seeds are in an apple, but only God can tell you how many apples are in a seed."

You're probably thinking—huh? What does that mean? You could walk into any classroom, nursery, business meeting, or home down the street, and start counting people, or seeds as Reva called them. But there is no way you can possibly know the amount of potential in each of those seeds! Jesus once said that whoever calls someone a "fool" is in danger of hell's fire. The word fool used in that verse comes from a Greek word meaning worthless or good for nothing. Never let anyone tell you what you are or are not capable of doing. The next time someone calls you a loser, prove them wrong. The next time someone tells you you're worthless, prove them wrong.

In 1977, Ken Olson—president, chairman, and founder of Digital Equipment Corporation—said, "There is no reason why anyone would want a computer in their home."

In my office hangs a picture with the following words written on it: "Everything that can be invented has been." Those were the words of our U.S. Patent Office in 1899. Thank goodness someone didn't believe that bunch of garbage.

As a freshman in college I took a Writing 101 class. Each day we were required to write a page in our journal. Throughout the semester we completed several lengthy pieces of work. One day, toward the end of that semester, we were quietly working in class when our instructor called me to the front. Everyone seemed to pause for a moment. It was uncommon for her to interrupt a class full of busy students. While everyone listened she said, "Jason, I've been watching you very carefully this semester and I'm convinced that you possess something marvelous." I thought, Wow! She went on to say, "You have the greatest writing problem that I have ever observed. Don't ever pursue a career in writing." I think I'll send her a copy of this book.

We are inspired by those who tear through the negativity of average folks. I've always heard that Walt Disney was fired from a newspaper job once. His employer told him that he lacked talent and creativity. Never be afraid to step out in faith. Remember that an amateur built the ark. A large group of professionals built the Titanic. One pessimist said, "I used to have an open mind, but then my brains fell out."

Psalm 1 promises that we will bear fruit in our season and whatsoever we do will prosper. Jesus said, "Every branch in Me will bear good fruit." Isaiah 54:17 says, "No weapon formed against me shall prosper, and every tongue which rises against me in judgment God shall condemn." Deuteronomy 28 says that I will be blessed in the city and blessed in the country, my children will be blessed, my property will be blessed, and my work will be blessed. I'll be blessed when I come and blessed when I go. He promises to defeat my enemies. Though they come at me one way, they will flee from me in seven different directions.

If you are a child of God, you are highly favored and blessed. Dream big and go for the gold. It's been said that a great oak is a little nut that held its ground. Go for it!

LOOKING INTO THE MIRROR

- What would you do if you were superhuman?

- Who would you save?

- What evil would you eradicate?

Labels and the Scars They Leave

I heard a story about a young boy who kept getting in trouble for picking on the other kids in his class. One night, his dad took him out to an old oak tree in their backyard. He handed the boy a bucket of rusty nails and a hammer. He said, "Son, every time you blow your top, fight, or push someone around, I want you to drive a nail in this old tree."

The next day he drove over twenty nails along the bottom of that tree. As the days went on, he hammered fewer nails. Two weeks later, the boy waited on the front porch for his father to come home from work. When his dad pulled into the driveway, he ran through the yard screaming, "Dad! Guess what? Guess what, Dad?" With a smile on his face, he said, "I didn't have to drive any nails into the tree today!"

His daddy patted him on the head and said, "Let me show you something, Son." The two of them stood in front of the nail-pierced tree. Nails cluttered the tree as far as that little boy could reach. For the next half hour he and his dad pulled out the rusty nails until the last one was removed. Then the dad set his son down and said, "Look at that old tree, Son. You can remove the nails, but you can never remove the scars." That's so true.

The Bible says that the power of life and death are in the tongue. James says that the tongue is set on fire by hell itself. God told the prophet Jeremiah that in his mouth, he had the power to uproot kingdoms or plant kingdoms, to build nations or destroy nations.

If you're the kind of person who gets a kick out of picking on someone else, the only moron is you. You never know; the person you push around now might someday own the company you will work for. Time has a way of turning the tables on us.

Anyone trying to achieve will be criticized and slandered from time to time. Over the years, I've made a list of encouraging thoughts that I often refer to when a dear soul finds something to criticize me over.

- Those who can, do. Those who can't, criticize.

- When I am right—nobody remembers. When I am wrong—nobody forgets.
- What will fault-finding people do in heaven?
- People who cut you down are only trying to reduce you to their size.

LOOKING INTO THE MIRROR

Author Laurie Beth Jones in her book, *The Path*, talks about the power of prophecies, both positive and negative.

- Make a list of positive words that have been spoken to you or about you.

        Positive   Negative

- Next, take any negative words that stand out in your mind and compare them to what God's Word says about you. For example, look at the list of verses at the end of the section titled "The Pride of Suicide."

Fighting for Your Destiny

Acts 7:22 says that Moses was learned in all the wisdom of the Egyptians and was mighty in words and deeds. Mighty in words? When God called Moses, his number one argument with God was over his so-called inability to speak. The Word of God said that Moses was mighty in words, but we hear something completely different coming from the mouth of Moses. When we talk about our gifting, we often become our own worst enemy. In some cases, it doesn't matter how much God believes in us or how much the people around us believe in us; if we fail to believe in ourselves, we will always live beneath our full potential.

For many years, Israel had lived in Egyptian bondage, and God was asking (or telling) Moses to go lead them out. Despite his insecurities, the Bible says, "It came into his heart to visit his people, the children of Israel" (Acts 7:23).

When God gives you an opportunity to succeed, it always starts with an idea, a "coming into the heart moment" like in Moses' case. We fail to go to another level when we procrastinate by over spiritualizing things. We start wondering, "Is this idea really God or is this just my own wild idea? How do I know if this is what God wants me to do?" Forget about all that stuff. If you have a good idea that can benefit others, run with it! I would rather fail by trying, than fail by doing nothing at all! In Jesus' parable of the talents, the only servant He rebuked was the one who did nothing with what he was given. Take every idea as if God authored it. Realize that not all your ideas are your ideas. If the same mind that was in Christ Jesus is also in you (Philippians 2:5), then our thoughts are His thoughts and His thoughts ours.

Notice verses 25–27 of Acts 7: "And seeing one of them suffer wrong, he defended and avenged him who opposed, and struck down the Egyptian. For he supposed that his brethren would have understood that God would deliver them by his hand, but they did not understand."

Let this be a lesson to us; not everyone will understand our dreams, and not everyone will agree with our dreams. Sometimes we have to be careful who we share our dreams with. Some folks are in the ministry of misery. Their years of doing nothing has brought them much bitterness and pessimism. They only point out what is fearful, doubtful, and negative. Some folks see opportunity while others only see the obstacles.

One of the great preachers of church history was Dwight L. Moody. After Moody moved to Chicago, he asked a struggling church's Sunday school superintendent if he could help teach a class. The man said, "We have twelve teachers now and only sixteen students attending. We don't need your help. What we need are more eager students." That's all Moody needed to hear. The next Sunday Moody showed up with eighteen young people. He walked right up to the Sunday school superintendent and said, "I've got you some new boys, mister, not very many I'm afraid, but they've all got souls that need to be saved." Before Moody went to be with the Lord, he preached to over 100 million people throughout the world.

When John Wesley began preaching in England, his simple enthusiastic style of preaching was rejected by the Church of England. He traveled to America and preached to the Indians. A few years later, he set sail again and preached to the unchurched masses of Britain. Before Wesley died, he traveled over 250,000 miles during the 1700s. He preached over 42,000 sermons, wrote over 200 pieces of material, and he is considered the spiritual father of more than thirty-five denominations, including the Methodist, Wesleyan, Pentecostal, Nazarene, Holiness, and modern charismatic movements.

I've noticed that when someone dreams of greatness, everyone snickers; but, when he or she achieves something great, everyone claims they had something to do with it. Several years ago, I came across the following story:

> Late one night in the insane asylum one inmate shouted, "I am Napoleon!"
> Another yelled, "I'm going to be the next pope!"
> Across the hall someone asked, "How do you know you're going to be the next pope?"
> "Because, God told me," the man said.
> Just then a voice from the next room shouted, "I did not!"

In life, there are many voices. We must silence the critics and fine tune our ears to the voice of the Holy Spirit. Be like the boxer who was counted out several times, but never heard the referee.

LOOKING INTO THE MIRROR

Joan of Arc heard voices and was labeled a heretic; later she was heralded a hero.

- Right now in your life, what voices have your attention? Be brutally honest!

No More Talking About It

P aul introduces himself in the book of Romans as one who is "called to be an apostle." He begins his first letter to the church of Corinth the same way.

"Paul, called to be an apostle of Jesus Christ . . ." (1 Corinthians 1:1).

Then we come to 2 Corinthians 1:1 and he says something much different about himself. He says, "I am Paul, an apostle of Jesus Christ . . ." No longer is he talking about what he will be, or what he hopes to be. He has moved from "wanting to be" to "being." He is no longer dreaming about what his apostleship will look like. He has stepped into his calling. There are those who talk about doing great things, and there are those who do great things. We all know talk is cheap!
Have you ever dreamed up a really awesome gizmo and a year later saw it on the shelf at Walmart? I've done it a hundred times. At some point, I realized that the only difference between me and that other guy was fear and procrastination. Someone just like me decided to take a risk, to step out, even though he or she didn't have all the questions answered. I remember reading a t-shirt once that said: "A life lived in fear is a life half lived." I keep a little note on file that says: "Stop praying for an oak tree when there are acorns all around you. Your ideas are the tiny acorns from which great oaks grow." Those crazy ideas are God's way of introducing you to your destiny.
A great way to discern your purpose is to consider your passions. Our passions can reveal to us our purpose. What are you most passionate about? If you knew that you would not fail, what would you attempt to do today? Years ago, I decided to follow through with every idea regardless of what became of it. What God chose to do with it would be His business. I'll do my part and wait on Him to do His.
Someone once said that the two greatest days in your life is the day you are born and the day you find out why. Winston Churchill said, "There comes a special moment in everyone's life, a moment for which that person was born. That special opportunity,

when he seizes it, will fulfill his mission—a mission for which he is uniquely qualified. In that moment, he finds greatness. It is his finest hour." Discovering your purpose is one thing, but living it out is entirely different.

In Romans 1:1, Paul says that he was "separated unto the Gospel." In other words, he focused only on that which he knew he was called to. You can be good at a lot of things and be great at nothing. Remember, God has called us to be fruitful, not busy. Instead of trying to be the best at everything, concentrate on being your best at the one or two things that you're greatest at. If Paul had not learned to separate himself to his calling, he would have died unfulfilled. His life would have ended in regret.

It's also important that we realize that the more the responsibility, the less the options. The opposite is also true; the less the responsibility, the more the options. In high school, you can play every sport, take dance classes, art classes, guitar lessons, hang out at the mall with your friends, and the list could keep on going. However, if you're going to be the next legendary Major-League baseball player, you will be forced to let go of something. The closer you get to the dream, the more focused you must become.

LOOKING INTO THE MIRROR

- What is the difference between a model and a mold?

Sex and Secrets

I wake from the sweet dreams of my love
In the first breath of my awakening I taste her breath
Laying silent in a daze
With the moon's light beaming down upon my bed
My eyes dazzling with amazement
As I imagine my love dancing around the bed
In the glory of the almighty Father with all the angels of heaven
Rejoicing as they gaze upon the perfection of beauty
I hear a melody . . .
The sound of her voice tickling my ears
As the sound ventures down the hallway of my lifeless home
I realize that I am alone
My love has yet to appear
For I am still waiting

By Jamie Jones

Hidden Habits

Perhaps the greatest reason we lack confidence is our lack of character. It's hard to feel good about yourself if you're a liar. The only thing worse than being criticized is knowing that your accuser is telling the truth.

I never was good at getting away with things growing up. Somehow, I always got caught. My uncle gave me his Cutlass Oldsmobile when I was fifteen years old. It sat covered up at the end of our driveway. One night, my buddy and I decided to sneak it out while my parents were gone. I pulled the cover off the car, hopped in the driver's seat, and took off. We weren't planning on robbing a bank or anything. We just wanted to cruise down the road and back. No one would even notice, or so I thought! Apparently, I didn't pull the car's cover off all the way. It had snagged on the edge of the back bumper. So, while we sailed down U.S. HWY 119, behind us flew this dumb-looking parachute. When I got home, there was barely anything left of the cover. My middle name should have been "Busted."

The truth is there are no secrets. God sees everything. Notice the following verses:

"If we had forgotten the name of our God, or stretched out our hands to a foreign god, would not God search this out? For He knows the secrets of the heart" (Psalm 44:20-21).

"O God, You know my foolishness; and my sins are not hidden from You" (Psalm 69:5)

"For we have been consumed by Your anger, and by Your wrath we are terrified. You have set our iniquities before You, our secret sins in the light of Your countenance" (Psalm 90:7-8).

Everything done in darkness will be brought to light, and everything whispered in secret will be proclaimed from the house tops. However, God offers mercy wherever there's honesty. If we will come clean, God will clean us up. A great preacher once said that whatever we uncover, God will always cover. The flipside is also true; whatever we cover, God will eventually uncover.

If there are any hidden habits in your life, stop meddling in that junk. Let God deal with the secrets in your life—don't hide anything. Drag it out there in the open. Pull the cover off of it and cry out to God. Experience His forgiveness and He will wash away the guilt and fill your life with freedom and power.

LOOKING INTO THE MIRROR

- Secrecy gives power to shame. Can you think of a Bible story that validates this statement?

- Think of a time when you did something as a kid and tried to hide it. What had you done?

- Did you get busted?

- What happened when you got busted?

- How did the cover up affect the outcome?

The Third Commandment

Don't take the name of the Lord in vain—a simple to understand, straight forward commandment. Don't say "Jesus" when you bump your toe, and never put our God's name before a bad word. Though these examples are worthy of following, I wonder if the commandment is broader than the obvious.

I believe this commandment could apply to the walking, breathing contradictions that we often are. I would then paraphrase the third commandment like this: "Don't take the name of our Lord and live a life of selfish vanity." Maybe this would do better: "Don't take the Father's name only to become an embarrassment to the family of God." One thing is for sure, this commandment is not just about words we say, but about the lives we live.

Growing up around church I was accustomed to hearing people share what the preacher called "a testimony." A testimony is one's personal story of salvation, very similar to a testimony given in a courtroom. A believer's testimony is his or her story of what happened before, during, and after he or she met Christ.

I loved hearing the "good testimonies." The worse the story was, the better the testimony. My definition of a "good testimony" was like an R-rated movie that ended with, "Then I met Jesus." Of course, my views would later change. After all, what is better—to steal and stop stealing or to never steal?

The truth is we all have two testimonies: the one we tell and the one we live. When the one we tell does not agree with the one we live, then our testimony falters. Our lives become a stumbling block to those around us. Those standing outside the church associate Christianity with hypocrisy. When what we claim to be lines up with what others know us to be, we then have a great testimony.

LOOKING INTO THE MIRROR

If you're a Christian, then ask yourself the following questions:

- Do my choices take the name of the Lord in vain?

- Do the two testimonies in my life agree?

Coming Out from Among God's People

The book of Judges tells us the story of a guy named Gideon. God had given His people (Israel) a great land and He had blessed their land; but, they got a little comfortable and began drifting away from the Lord. Now, when we drift away from the Lord, we drift away from His blessings, His promises, His provision, His peace, His joy, His rest, and so on. The further they traveled from God, the further they traveled from His benefits. They gave themselves to idol worship and when they did, their defense was gone. A group of nomadic raiders, called the Midianites, invaded their land.

The people of God were pushed into the mountains surrounding their homeland. They looked out of the caves and through the trees and watched the Midianites plunder their properties. The Midianites ate their food, lived in their homes, drank their wine, and lived off their livestock. The Midianites were without number; they were like a swarm of locusts, the Bible says—too many to count.

This wasn't the first time the Midianites appeared in God's Word. Joseph was sold to a group of Midianites and they sold Joseph as a slave to the Egyptians. The Midianites were distant relatives to Israel, descendants of Abraham's son, Midian. They wandered the deserts living off the lands they conquered. Once again, the people of God had become their target.

It was during this time that Gideon was met by an angel. In Judges 6:12, the angel said, "The Lord is with you, you mighty man of valour." Every time I've heard a message about Gideon, he is referred to as a wimp and here's why. When the angel first appeared to Gideon, he was threshing wheat inside a winepress. Now, normally you would thresh wheat out in an open space called a threshing floor, but because of the Midianite invasion, Gideon was threshing his wheat in a hidden place. However, Gideon was not a wimp! Gideon was brave enough to come out of his cave, go down the mountain, and walk out of the forest. He was tired of the enemy taking what belonged to him and his people, so on he went!

Back to his daddy's home place. Back to his daddy's wheat. Back to his daddy's barn.

He didn't have the guts to take on the entire Midianite mob, but he did have the guts to reclaim what was his. Have you ever given something away and after it was gone, you wanted it back? That's what Israel did. They drifted away from God and as a result, they gave their land away; but Gideon came along and said, "Hey boys, I want my stuff back."

While everyone else hid, Gideon stepped out. He was different from the rest of God's people. The day of stepping out from among the world is over. There's a new day upon us. Today, God is calling us to step out from among the church. It's time to be different than the average church-goer. There's not much difference between the kids at the party and the kids at church these days. Jesus didn't lay down His life so that you and I could earn a "perfect attendance Sunday School Award." Jesus laid down His life so that we might be free from the power of sin.

The angel also told Gideon that God was going to use him to defeat the Midianites. But Gideon had a hard time seeing himself as the mighty warrior that God said he was.

Now, before Gideon could deal with his enemies, first he had to deal with something in his own home. You see, Gideon had a big idol in his backyard that his father had built. God told Gideon he had to remove the idol before he could take on the Midianites. So, before he could triumph in his public life, he had to triumph in his private life. The Bible says, "When my ways please the Lord . . . (Private Life) . . . then God will make my enemies be at peace with me . . . (Public Life)." Someone once said, "You can't stand against the devil if you're not sure how you stand with God!"

Gideon tore down his daddy's idol and in its place he built an altar. What a message! It is in our hearts as fallen, insecure people to build idols around our success. We, like Lucifer, want to exalt ourselves. At my idol, I find significance; but at an altar, all I find is death. However, it's only when I decrease that Christ is allowed to increase in my life, and that is true success!

LOOKING INTO THE MIRROR

Let me ask you a few questions. Write down the answers to these questions and be totally honest.

- Is there something in your backyard that you need to tear down? If so, what is it?

- Are you hiding something in the closet that you need to throw on an altar? If so, what is it?

- When's the last time you laid your flesh on the altar?

- What happened?

- When's the last time you said, "God I present myself to you as a living sacrifice?"

Little Things that Make a Big Difference

For years I went to school with a devil kid named . . . well, let's just call him Billy. If Billy wasn't demon possessed, the devil sure missed a good opportunity. For a couple years, we were in the Boy Scouts together. One weekend, while camping at Kingdom Come State Park, our troop leader decided to take us all boating. Billy and his gang of thugs climbed into a boat, pushed off, paddled out in the lake, pulled the plug, and you guessed it, they sank the boat! From there the details are fuzzy, but I don't believe Billy earned his Eagle Scout badge.

A few weeks ago, I was reorganizing my storage closet at the church. I moved a box off one of the shelves, and there on the shelf sat a small little boat plug. Where it came from, I'll probably never know; but the moment I saw it, I was reminded of how important the little things are. Little things sure make a big difference.

Now, think about Adam and Eve's story. God placed Adam and Eve in the Garden of Eden and surrounded them with the beauty of His creation. During the cool of each day, God visited with the two of them. Adam and Eve literally "hung out" face to face with God. Each evening, they walked the garden with the creator of the universe. God gifted them and encouraged their creativity. They became God's partners in creation. Adam tended the garden and gave each animal its own, unique name. There was only one thing that God asked Adam to refrain from. "Don't eat from the tree of the knowledge of good and evil," God said.

I'm sure you know the story. Satan deceived Eve with his craftiness. While Adam watched, Eve took a bite. Many folks have wondered why Adam let Eve take that bite. Maybe he thought, If she eats and lives, then I'll take a bite too. If she dies . . . well, I've got a few more ribs and I would kind of like to see what a redhead looks like.

What we do know is the Bible says that they both ate. One bite changed everything! Before the fall of man, everything—beast, bird, and man—lived off vegetation. Nothing ever craved meat.

"And God said, 'See, I have given you every herb that yields seed which is on the face of all the earth, and every tree whose fruit yields seed; to you it shall be for food. Also, to every beast of the earth, to every bird of the air, and to everything that creeps on the earth, in which there is life, I have given every green herb for food;' and it was so" (Genesis 1:29-30).

God told Adam that the day he ate of the tree he would die. Adam didn't realize that the day he ate, everything would die. I've learned that God seldom tells us everything. Once Adam took that one little bite, sin was released into the earth's atmosphere and everything changed. From that moment on, creation turned on itself and everything became blood thirsty. Why was there a thirst for blood? The Bible says, "Without the shedding of blood there can be no forgiveness of sin." Every time Adam saw a bird swoop down and pluck a worm out of the ground, he was reminded of his sin.

For too long we have belittled the seriousness of sin. My pastor always says, "We can choose our sin, but we cannot choose the consequences of our sin." Adam learned the hard way that the little things are a big deal. According to a January Fox News survey conducted in 2005, the average American lies over 88,000 times during his or her lifetime. That's a lot of little white lies isn't it?

A great myth we often buy into is that our sin only affects us. All of creation suffered because of Adam's sin. Our choices shape the world around us. After he ate that one little bite, he hid. His shame forced him into isolation. When God came down to visit that evening, things looked quite a bit different.

LOOKING INTO THE MIRROR

- Imagine what might have happened had Adam and Eve ran to meet God when He came looking for them. What would have been different?

- Think about the dialog between Satan and those he tempted.

    Satan to Eve, "What's the big deal; it's just a piece of fruit?"
    Satan to Jesus, "What's the big deal; it's just a piece of bread?"

    What *is* the deal?

- The deadly fruit came from a tree called the Tree of Knowledge of Good and Evil. What was so bad about knowing good and evil?

Peace, Joy, and Rest

The words peace, joy, and rest appear in the Bible 807 times. These three things are directly connected to living a life that honors God. The closer I get to Jesus the more I will experience these three things in my life. Doctors have indicated that 70–85 percent of all physical ailments are provoked by emotional disturbance. Such debilitating diseases as heart trouble, high blood pressure, ulcers, asthma, some forms of arthritis, and so on, derive from emotional stress. In the book *None of These Diseases*, Dr. McMillian lists fifty-one diseases that are linked to emotional distress. Have you ever been so bummed out that you felt physically sick?

Ups and downs are a part of life. However, long seasons of depression or anxiety are not healthy, nor are they the will of God. The National Center for Health Statistics reports that almost 1 million people a year lose their lives to diseases caused by unmanaged stress. To cope, we now ingest 60,000 pounds of aspirins, tranquilizers, and sleeping pills a day.[4]

Some folks have bought into the assumption that the more stuff you've got, the more joy you've got. There's an old saying that goes: "He who dies with the most toys is still dead." The truth is Jesus is the key to happiness. The Bible says, "In the presence of God there is fullness of joy." I've been to about every unbelievable place the world has to offer, but there is no place as wonderful as in God's presence. If you're depressed and perplexed, you may not need more medication. What you really need is a visitation from the Spirit of God. Believe it or not, He is much closer than you're aware of; He is only a whisper away.

The Bible calls King David "a man after God's heart." However, David's life was far from perfect. One evening, he was walking on the roof of the palace. As he looked off the edge, he noticed a beautiful woman bathing. Lust gripped his heart and he sent his men to get her. The affair led to more devious deeds. Soon he had her husband set up and killed. During this season of David's life, he was filled with depression. For a period of time, he didn't eat. The following passage is from a song David wrote during those days:

"Have mercy upon me, O God, according to the multitude of Your tender mercies, blot out my transgressions. Wash me thoroughly from my iniquity, and cleanse me from my sin. For I acknowledge my transgressions, and my sin is always before me. Against You, You only, have I sinned, and done this evil in Your sight—that You may be found just when You speak, and blameless when You judge. Behold, I was brought forth in iniquity, and in sin my mother conceived me. Behold, You desire truth in the inward parts, and in the hidden part You will make me to know wisdom. Purge me with hyssop, and I shall be clean; wash me, and I shall be whiter than snow. Make me hear joy and gladness, that the bones You have broken may rejoice. Hide Your face from my sins, and blot out all my iniquities. Create in me a clean heart, O God, and renew a steadfast spirit within me. Do not cast me away from Your presence, and do not take Your Holy Spirit from me. Restore to me the joy of Your salvation, and uphold me by Your generous Spirit. Then I will teach transgressors Your ways, and sinners shall be converted to You" (Psalm 51:1-13).

Obviously, David realized that the joy he once knew came from the presence of the Lord and a clean heart before God. Someone once said, "The softest pillow to lay your head on at night is a clean conscience." Being in God's presence is one thing, but being in God's presence with a clean heart is something entirely different. After David returned to the Lord, joy returned to David. Repentance leads to refreshing.

An old Italian proverb says that where the river is deepest, it is the calmest. When our lives are deeply saturated in prayer and the Word of God, then we will experience peace that surpasses all understanding. In the fourth chapter of the book of Revelation, John describes the atmosphere around the throne of God. From His throne proceeds lightning, thunder, and voices. There are angels crying out, elders bowing down, the hosts of heaven singing, creatures roaring, and in the midst of all that commotion, there's a crystal sea. Not a sea of crystals, but a sea so calm that it looks more like a solid than a liquid. You see, in the presence of God there is all kinds of activity, yet there is complete serenity.

Whatever is going on in your life today, I pray that you will experience the calmness of His presence and the joy brought by a pure heart before God.

LOOKING INTO THE MIRROR

- Think of an acronym for R.E.S.T.

    R

    E

    S

    T

- According to the Strong's Exhaustive Concordance, the word pure means clean. Clean comes from a word that means to be bare. What does this mean to you?

Porn and Dirty Little Secrets

Webster's definition of pornography is writing, photography, film, etc., that creates sexual desire. We think of porn as seductive nudity. But porn is anything that gets your mind and your body cranked up for sex, such as the Victoria Secret's store in your local mall. If you don't intentionally look the other way, before you know it, you've allowed your eyes to travel all over the poster model's body or at least glanced at her breasts. Some may argue, but my friend, that's pornography. We've become so desensitized by the content of most television shows, movies, commercials, billboards, and general advertisements, that we don't even realize how deep the seduction is. Job said that he made a covenant with his eyes not to look at a woman to lust after her (see Job 31:1). Jesus said, ". . . if your eye offends you, pluck it out. It would be better to enter into heaven with one eye then to be cast into hell with both of them." He also said that our eyes are the windows of our soul (see Matthew 6:22–23).

- 720 million porn movies are watched every year.
- Studies vary, but we do know that Americans spend somewhere between $8-12 billion annually on porn.
- 37 percent of pastors say online pornography is a struggle for them.[5]

Following porn are all the hidden habits—900 numbers, masturbation, cyber sex, and the sins go deeper and deeper. Many justify their behavior by constantly reminding themselves that they are not actually having sex with someone. Some young people will even claim sexual purity despite their addiction to these secret sins. In the book of Isaiah, the prophet foretells of the coming Christ. He says that a virgin shall conceive and give birth to the Messiah (Isaiah 7:14). In this passage, the word virgin originates from the Hebrew word *alam*, which is pronounced, "aw-lam." This Hebrew word means to veil from sight, conceal, blind, hide, keep secret, keep out of sight, or keep private. In other words, a virgin is someone whose body has never been willfully touched and looked upon in a sexual manner.

God's idea of virginity is so much different from ours. So many young people think they're pure because they've never "gone all the way." Yet they've let a dozen dates kiss and rub all over them. That's not God's idea of purity.

These sins carry a weighty guilt along with them. Pretty soon you're no longer able to look at yourself in the mirror. You're left with a dirtiness that eats at your soul. With each encounter, more innocence is lost. You start to ask the question, "Is this really a sin or not?" Your lack of confidence should be enough to answer the question, but you ask it anyway. Think about it. The Holy Spirit brings into our lives joy, peace, rest, confidence, etc. Any habit in our lives that robs us of those things should be confessed and repented of. One of the greatest weapons of your defense will be total honesty and serious accountability. Be honest with God and confess it all as the sin that it is. Then make yourself accountable to someone you can trust.

LOOKING INTO THE MIRROR

- Sara Groves wrote a song that says, "Honesty is the only thing that can save us now." How can honesty save us?

- Can you think of a high-profile scandal in which lies were exposed? What is there to learn from that experience?

Are You Alone?

Alone—it's perhaps the most despised word in the English language. However, the word alone originates from two words: all—one. Drop one l and smash the two words together and you have the word alone. The word alone is essential for healthy living. It amazes me how so many people seek contentment in the game of dating. Have you ever known someone who just couldn't live without a boyfriend or a girlfriend? They have this ridiculous fear of being alone. Most people don't need to find a date; they need to find a life.

Only when you are first alone (all one) are you ready to bring someone else in the picture. One of my favorite speakers, Louie Giglio, once said, "The goal in life is not to find someone, but to become someone worth finding." Amen Louie!

The Bible says that we are complete in Christ. A companion may compliment you, but a companion will never complete you. As my friend once told his daughter, "You should get so lost in Christ that a boy would have to seek God to find you." The irony of dating is that it often fuels the sense of loneliness instead of curing it. With dating comes dumping and with dumping comes rejection and with rejection comes loneliness. In most cases, dating is practicing for divorce. Dating prepares us for bitter breakups more than lasting companionship. There's nothing wrong with dating; it's the way we date that's so off track.

Melissa and I have been married since 1996, and we've been serving in youth ministry together from day one. It's no telling how many young couples we've talked with about marriage. We've even talked a few out of it! I'll never forget one eighteen-year-old girl who stopped by to announce that she was getting married the upcoming weekend. Melissa and I were shocked because we didn't realize she was dating anyone. I asked her how long she had been seeing this fellow. "About two months," she said. "How old is he?" I asked. She said that he was twenty-three. My next question was, "What does he do for a living?" She said, "He isn't working at the time, but he is looking." I kept hammering the questions until I discovered that he hadn't worked in two years, he wasn't going to school, and he was living with his grandmother. Whoever said that you could live off love must not have lived very long. There in our living room sat a sweet, beautiful, young lady who was about to marry someone whose life was headed nowhere. The last thing that twenty-three-year-old guy needed was a wife.

Work on becoming alone. Set some goals for yourself. Get your life moving in a direction. Then, and only then, are you ready to share your life with somebody.

LOOKING INTO THE MIRROR

- Why do people fear being alone? List as many reasons as you can in the space below.

- Usually, at the root of fear is a lie. Is it possible to tell part of the truth without lying?

- Is telling only part of the truth the same thing as being honest?

- Is it possible to choose your words so carefully that you don't technically lie, but at the same time, you avoid being honest?

- Is there a difference between being honest and telling the truth?

Dumping Your Date

Wherever there's dating, there will be dumping. Where one is, the other is just around the corner. In Matthew 18, Jesus says that if someone caused one of His little ones to stumble, it would be better for a millstone to be hung around his neck, and he were drowned in the depths of the sea. In other words, Jesus gets extremely ticked off when someone hurts one of His children! Most people don't think about that when they're dumping their date. Paul reminds us in Romans 12:19 that vengeance belongs to the Lord and He will repay. That's serious stuff! So let's think about how we should and should not end a dating relationship. Let's look at four "don't do's" when dumping:

1. Don't let him or her talk you back into the relationship.

Now, in some cases, this may be a rule we can "fudge on." However, if you had major issues before, things probably won't be any different this time around. I once knew a young couple who had been together for a few years. They were engaged and had set the wedding date. Their relationship had experienced its fair share of ups and downs. One day they were in love and the next day they hated each other. So I told them, "Dating is kind of like looking into your car's side mirror. Have you ever noticed that little sticker that says, 'Objects are much larger than they appear?' That's exactly how it is when you date someone. The little things that bother you now, don't go away. They get bigger!" I couldn't tell you how many times I've watched a couple break it off, get back together, think it will be different this time, walk down the aisle, have children, and divorce. Don't get caught in that trap. Move on!

2. Don't prolong the breakup.

If the goal of dating is to find the person you're going to spend the rest of your life with, and it's obvious the person you're dating is not "the one," then don't put off what you know is coming. Some people stay in a relationship that's headed nowhere because they don't want to hurt the other person's feelings. On one hand that may sound noble. Actually, it's cruel and it's called being a tease. The longer you draw out the process, the more painful it will be and the more long-term damage it will cause.

3. Don't blame God.

Guys, don't tell a girl that God told you to dump her, or vice versa. It sounds like you and God have been talking bad about your girlfriend. It's like God doesn't think she deserves you or that God thinks you're better than she is. Don't sign God's name to the Dear John letter. If He wasn't a part of the hookup, don't make Him a part of the breakup!

4. Don't let dating and dumping destroy the relationships around you.

If there's one thing I hate, it's drama. God's not too fond of it either. Proverbs 6 says God hates those who sow discord. Whether you do the dumping or you get dumped, don't run your mouth and talk trash about your "ex." That won't solve anything, nor will it change the fact that you're no longer together. Bite your tongue if necessary. Proverbs 16:32 says, "He who is slow to anger is better than the mighty, and he who rules his spirit than he who takes a city." Proverbs 25:28 says, "Whoever has no rule over his own spirit is like a city broken down, without walls." Psalm 1 describes the downward digression of someone whose life is gripped by wickedness. Sin reaches full bloom when the individual is sitting in the seat of the scornful. We are as far away from God as we can get when we are sitting in that seat. Discord is a sure sign that someone is disconnected from God.

I heard a story once about a guy who broke up with his girlfriend before he left for college. The next weekend, she was out with someone else. A few weeks later, she emailed him and asked for her pictures. He rounded up dozens of photos of old girlfriends and a few guys from the dorm threw in some of their own girlfriends' pictures. In the package he put in a note that read: "Dear Jill, pick out the pictures that belong to you. I'm sorry, but I forgot what you looked like."

VERSES TO THINK UPON:

"Whoever hides hatred has lying lips, and whoever spreads slander is a fool" (Proverbs 10:18).

"For wherever there is jealousy and selfish ambition, there you will find disorder and evil of every kind. But the wisdom from above is first of all pure. It is also peace loving, gentle at all times, and willing to yield to others. It is full of mercy and good deeds. It shows no favoritism and is always sincere. And those who are peacemakers will plant seeds of peace and reap a harvest of righteousness" (James 3:16-18, New Living Translation).

LOOKING INTO THE MIRROR

- At some point or another, most of us have heard a classic breakup line. Take a few minutes and compile a list of your favorites.

- How do you know it is time to get out of the relationship?

- Once you've become sexually active with someone it's much harder to end the relationship. How would you advise someone in this situation?

Sex-Esteem

Proverbs 6:32 says, "But the man who commits adultery (sex outside of marriage) is an utter fool, for he destroys himself. He will be wounded and disgraced. His shame will never be erased" (New Living Translation).

In our years of youth ministry, Melissa and I have met with numerous young men and women after they lost their virginity. The thrill itself was nothing to compare to the emptiness that followed. Of course, I know there are plenty of young people who look for sexual opportunities, but in many cases, things get out of control and two people end up "going places" they were not intending to go. We've sat in our living room many times and watched young men and women cry their eyes out, wishing they could take back what they had done.

First of all let me say that sex is not bad. God thought it up! He made man and woman and commanded them to "be fruitful and multiply" or have children. It's difficult to have children without having sex. Sex was and is God's plan. According to scripture, the bed of a married couple is holy (see Hebrew 13:4). However, God always intended for sex to be enjoyed within the boundaries of marriage. It's when we have sex outside of the way God intended that we get in trouble. Sex then becomes sin. The greatest sexual experience that you can ever have is within the context of marriage. The greatest gift you can give your spouse is your sexual innocence.

In the book, *Questions You Can't Ask Your Mama About Sex*, the authors make the following statement: "Repeatedly the Bible says not to be sexually immoral. The Bible does not say just to avoid the act of sexual intercourse outside of marriage, but to avoid sexual immorality. In other words, God wants us to be sexually pure."

Over the last century, our definition of sexual purity has become so vague. Looking back to the Clinton days, our president swore under oath: "I did not have sexual relations with that woman," but that depends on your definition of "sexual relations." Rolling around, body to body, on the floor simulating the full act of sexual intercourse without "doing it" is still what I consider a sexual experience. The fact that there is a thin layer of clothing between the two of you does not make this a God-blessed act.

In our sex-driven society, it can be difficult to keep our minds out of the gutter. However, we cannot blame our sexual battles on our environment. Adam had a perfect environment, but he still sinned. God gave him a beautiful woman to be his wife. The two of them walked around naked all day long, then spent every evening with God. Now that's every young man's dream right there! Adam didn't struggle with lust or porn, because Eve was the only woman on the earth. However, even in that environment, Adam sinned.

On the flip side, we have Daniel, a Jewish captive living in the dark Babylonian Empire. Babylon provided one of the most ungodly environments the world has ever known. Yet, in the middle of such wickedness, this young man had an excellent spirit. When everyone else bowed their knees to the pressures around them, Daniel lived upright. In all that he did, he honored God. He lived in the world, but not like the world. His parents were killed and his homeland destroyed, and he had every reason to make excuses for his weaknesses. All the odds were stacked against him. After a law was passed prohibiting prayer, Daniel got in the window facing Jerusalem and prayed three times a day. Nothing could derail this young man. It's no wonder God showed up in the lions' den. God will always reward righteousness. God will always display His might when we do what's right.

Set boundaries around your dating life. Don't allow yourself to get in a compromising situation. Go on group dates. Surround yourself with accountability. Make your convictions known before you even think about getting into a serious relationship with someone.

LOOKING INTO THE MIRROR

- We are creatures of benefit and consequence. Read the first chapter of Daniel. What were some of the benefits of Daniel's choices?

He Loves Me . . . He Loves Me Not

Second Samuel 13 tells the story of a beautiful girl named Tamar who was raped by her half brother Amnon. Eaten up with lust, Amnon shared his feelings with his twisted cousin, Jonadab. A plan was formulated and Amnon did the unthinkable. Jonadab told Amnon to pretend to be sick, to ask Tamar to serve him dinner in bed, to lock the door behind her, and to take her. Amnon did just as Jonadab advised.

Before the rape took place, Amnon repeatedly said that he was in love with Tamar, but after he got what he wanted, the Bible said that he hated her exceedingly. Scripture says, "The hatred with which he hated her was greater than the love which he had loved her. And Amnon told her, 'Arise, and be gone!'" One minute he loved her, the next minute he loved her not! The truth is he never loved her. He loved sex.

Girls, if you're dating a guy who only tells you that he loves you when he is all over you, you need to run as fast as you can. He doesn't love you, he loves how you make him feel; and there are a million other girls who can make him feel that way. Tamar's naiveté cost her dearly. According to the Children's Defense Fund, every day in America 3,742 babies are born to unmarried mothers. That means every two minutes and forty seconds, some guy is telling some girl how special she is and after he gets what he wants, he's gone!

Several years ago my wife took a group of high-school girls through an incredible book entitled *Girls of Grace*. The book is filled with questions that teenage girls have emailed Christian celebrities. One girl writes, "All of my life people have told me I should stay a virgin until I get married. I've been with my boyfriend for about three months, and when we are together he makes me feel special. He wants to go further and sometimes I get lost in the moment and go there with him. How do I stop my feelings from allowing me to go too far?" Another girl says, "I am going out with the most wonderful guy. He's so perfect for me. We like the same things—like movies, music, sports, and we even have the same favorite foods and color! But more than all that, I love the way he makes me feel that I am special—he says that nobody has ever made him feel the way I make him feel. The only problem I'm having in the relationship is the physical part. I'm afraid I've let things get out of control."

First of all, liking the same food and color doesn't mean anything. I have a good friend named Darrin. We both like Mexican food and the color black, but I'm not going to make out with him. My buddy David and I both like old cars and strawberry cake but the first time he tries to kiss me I'm breaking his nose. Girls, a boy will learn 4,000 Bible verses, join the church choir, and sing like a bird if he thinks it will better his chances of getting you this Friday night. Don't fall for that stuff. One young lady said that no one listens to her like her boyfriend does. Wolves do have big ears you know.

Allow me to drop a line or two about clothing. Girls, dressing trashy makes you attractive for sex, but not for marriage. In November of 1995, *Forbes* magazine featured an article titled, "You Are What You Wear." According to the article, the way you dress says everything about your character. If you've been accepted into God's kingdom, then you should dress acceptably.

Your typical teenage guy wants two girls: one to sleep with and one to marry who hasn't slept with anyone. You have to choose which girl you want to be. The bottom line is, if you want a good guy, be a good girl.

If you're out with a guy and he starts talking filthy, tell him to hit the road. To some it may just be another dirty joke; it's actually a test to see what makes you blush. How you respond says a lot. Walk wisely and trust the Lord. Set guidelines for the kind of guy you will or will not date. For starters, I tell teenagers all the time, "If that person is not a Christian, that person is not an option."

LOOKING INTO THE MIRROR

In the animal kingdom, the male is more decorative than the female. It is the male's instinct to spread his seed indiscriminately. He goes at it every chance he gets. But the female on the other hand is much different. Interestingly, the female instinctively saves her eggs. She keeps them for the most impressive male, so that her offspring will be the strongest and most distinct of their kind.

- What is the lesson to be learned here?

Somebody's Watching

In a Jewish marriage in the Old Testament, if the husband believed that his wife had been fooling around before they got married, the wife's family had to appear before the elders of Israel and present a case for her virginity. An investigation took place (see Deuteronomy 22:13–19). Let me ask you this question, "If your parents had to investigate your sexuality, what would they discover?"

According to a recent survey, 65 percent of sexually active teenagers said their parents think they are virgins. If your parents read your love notes, your text messages, your emails, visit your MySpace, overhear your conversations, and talk to your ex's, what will they find out about you?

Let's pretend that you have a hidden cameraman with you on all your dates. He captures everything that takes place and at the end of the night he follows you home. He sets up the projector, your mom pops the popcorn, your dad lounges in his favorite chair, grandma and grandpa come over, your little brother and sister gather around the screen, and everyone finds out what happens when someone goes out with you. If you knew that was going to happen, would you date differently? Believe it or not, that does happen. God's sees everything. The Bible says that we are surrounded by a great cloud of witnesses. Ask yourself, "When I walk away from a date, is my heart filled with the peace of God or conviction and uncertainty?"

Acts 21 tells of an evangelist named Phillip who had four virgin daughters who prophesied. One day I was wondering, "Why doesn't the Bible just say that Phillip had four daughters who prophesied?" Why do you think the scripture mentions their virginity? It's because their purity brought value to their ministry. Don't say, "Thus says the Lord," if you can't say, no to temptation. Listen, if you desire to be used by God, you must fight for your purity. The world has seen enough compromise within the Body of Christ. If you've made mistakes already, don't make them again. Jesus forgave the sin of a woman who was caught in bed with a man who was not her husband. He then said to her, "Now, go and sin no more."

LOOKING INTO THE MIRROR

My wife and I have a dear friend named Francis Brantley. Francis is one of those fiery grandmothers of the faith that God just didn't make enough of. She's been a blessing to my family for many years. For this section of "Looking into the Mirror," she has shared with us the following entry. Thanks Francis!

I once counseled with two different persons who were so perverted that they seemed unable to see the truth and the error of their ways. One, who had been married seven times, said she had never committed adultery—she married them all. The other one said she had never committed adultery because she was always faithful to the one she was sleeping with at the time.

- How do we get that deceived?

- Read 2 Timothy 3:1–7. What do you think verse seven means?

Pray this prayer with me, please. "Lord, thank You for revealing to me truth and grace. Truth shows me who I really am without You and who I really am with You. Truth shows me the dark places that I've covered up and hidden from myself and You. Only when I am completely honest will I ever really be free. When I am vulnerable and transparent, Your grace washes over me and cleanses me. I confess my need of You. Help me to be real. Show me the areas that I have ignored. Forgive me and cleanse me. Draw me into a deeper relationship with You. Make my hunger for You and Your word far greater than my hunger for anything else in this world. Thank You, Father. Amen."

The Esther Challenge

The crowning of Queen Esther is such a beautiful story. One day she was just another pitiful Jewish girl living under the oppression of the Great Persian Empire. Raised by her uncle, her parents were no doubt killed during the hostility of war. This young lady was among a race that was nearly exterminated during her lifetime. Yet overnight she became one of the most important figures in Jewish history. Let me remind you that Esther was the winning candidate of a highly publicized beauty pageant. Contestants of the pageant had to meet the following criteria:

1. Each young lady had to be beautiful.
2. Each young lady had to be a virgin.

It all started when the king of Persia threw a major party for all of the political leaders throughout his empire. The purpose of this celebration was to show off the wealth and splendor of his excellent majesty. It was a boasting party and it lasted 180 days! That was one big-headed king, my friend.

During the event, when the nobles were well drunk, the king commanded his wife to come "pole dance" for him and his boys. When she refused, the king was furious. Fearing the queen would start a trend among the women throughout the kingdom, he had her kicked out of the palace and banished from the empire. (At one time you could get away with things like that. Today, a good attorney would cost the king half of his kingdom—the better half!) Once the queen was gone, the search began. A new queen was needed.

"Then the king's servants who attended him said, 'Let beautiful young virgins be sought for the king; and let the king appoint officers in all the provinces of his kingdom, that they may gather all the beautiful young virgins . . .'" (Esther 2:2-3).

Young ladies from every city throughout the kingdom pranced before the king. Now the Persian Empire had conquered the Babylonian Empire, so this was not a small matter. Once the group was narrowed down, each lady went through a twelve-month preparation process before she appeared before the king. When it was all over, Esther was chosen.

Esther was a Jew but she told no one. Her uncle's name was Mordecai. The king's right-hand man was Haman. Haman despised Mordecai. No one in the palace knew the connection between Esther and Mordecai. Haman, knowing that Mordecai was a Jew, plotted to annihilate the entire Jewish race. Esther was oblivious to Haman's scheme and up until this point she wasn't that happy about being queen. But one night, Mordecai, said these words to her, "Esther, you've been given this honor for such a time as this." I think it would be safe to paraphrase his statement like this: "Esther, you've been given your beauty for such a time as this." You see, it is so important that we realize that God gives us our beauty and our talents based on trust. His hope is that in our moments of recognition, we will model His character and give Him glory. Today, our country is filled with celebrities who don't know how to be role models. More than ever before, America needs a celebrity with integrity.

- Someone to model beauty and holiness.
- Someone to model political authority and righteousness.
- Parents who will live respectful lives.
- Teachers who model godliness in and out of the classroom.
- Ministers who love God and people more than big crowds and large offerings.

These aren't sweet ideas and lofty thoughts, these are today's necessities.

I'm sure you know how the story ends:

- Esther prepared a meal for Haman and the king.
- She reminded the king of Haman's plan to destroy the Jews.
- She revealed to them both that she was a Jew.
- The king went off and—next thing you know—Haman was dead!
- The Jewish race was saved by the bravery of Queen Esther.

What saved Esther's people? Her virginity! Let me remind you that our Savior was a Jew. Had it not been for this young lady's commitment to save herself until marriage, we would all be without hope today. Her sexual purity saved her people and brought us Christ. God places a high honor upon those who wait. He used a virgin named Esther to save the Jews. He used a virgin named Mary to bring us the One who would ultimately save the world.

My dear friend, resist the temptations of this nasty world.

Fight for those watching you.

Honor the Lord with your body.

Please don't buckle under the pressure.

James 1:12 says, "Blessed is the man or woman who endures temptation; for when he has been approved, he will receive the crown of life which the Lord has promised to those who love Him."

LOOKING INTO THE MIRROR

- How can you prepare to resist in your time of temptation?

Dose of Truth

As a young man, I remember wondering what the Bible had to say about sex. I was far too lazy to search for the answers. Growing up, the only book I ever read was *Charley and the Chocolate Factory*. It was on a third-grade reading level. Several times I picked that book up. I loved the pictures but I kept getting stuck on a big word that appeared on page three. Reading was not my thing! No one ever talked about sex at church. Oh, we kids talked about it when the teacher stepped outside the classroom. I came to the conclusion that since most of my Sunday school teachers were extremely old, if they ever did have sex, they long forgot about it. Believe it or not, the Bible has a lot to say about sex. I've listed a few verses below to save you some time and trouble. Remember, Romans, 1 Corinthians, and 2 Timothy were all written by an unmarried man—a man with the same desires and passions the rest of us guys have.

"Keep me from sexual sins; let them not have dominion over me; then shall I be upright, and I shall be innocent from the great transgression" (Psalm 19:13).

"I will sing of mercy and justice; to You, O Lord, I will sing praises. I will behave wisely in a perfect way. Oh, when will You come to me? I will walk within my house with a perfect heart. I will set nothing wicked before my eyes; I hate the work of those who fall away; it shall not cling to me. A perverse heart shall depart from me; I will not know wickedness" (Psalm 101:1-4).

"The eyes of the Lord are in every place, beholding the evil and the good" (Proverbs 15:3, King James Version).

"Therefore God also gave them up to uncleanness, in the lusts of their hearts, to dishonor their bodies among themselves, who exchanged the truth of God for the lie, and worshipped and served the creature rather than the Creator, who is blessed forever. Amen. For this reason God gave them up to vile passions. For even their women exchanged the natural use for what is against nature. Likewise also the men, leaving the natural use of the woman, burned in their lust for one another, men with men committing what is shameful, and receiving in themselves the penalty of their error which was due. And even as they did not like to retain God in their knowledge, God gave them over to a debased mind, to do those things which are not fitting; being filled with all unrighteousness, sexual immorality, wickedness, covetousness, maliciousness, full of envy, murder, strife, deceit, evil-mindedness; they are whisperers, backbiters, haters of God, violent, proud, boasters, inventors of evil things, disobedient to parents, undiscerning, untrustworthy, unloving, unforgiving, unmerciful; who, knowing the righteous judgment of God, that those who practice such things are deserving of death, not only do the same but also approve of those who practice them" (Romans 1:24-32).

". . . make no provision for the flesh, to fulfill the lusts thereof" (Romans 13:14).

"Do you not know that the unrighteous will not inherit the kingdom of God? Do not be deceived. Neither fornicators (those having sex outside of marriage), nor idolaters, nor adulterers, nor homosexuals, nor sodomites, nor thieves, nor covetous, nor drunkards, nor revilers, nor extortioners will inherit the kingdom of God" (1 Corinthians 6:9).

". . . Now the body is not for fornication (sex outside of marriage), but for the Lord" (1 Corinthians 6:13).

"Flee fornication (sexual sin)" (1 Corinthians 6:18).

"For this you know, that no fornicator (someone having sex outside of marriage), unclean person, nor covetous man, who is an idolater, has any inheritance in the kingdom of Christ and God" (Ephesians 5:5).

"Flee youthful lusts" (2 Timothy 2:22).

"Marriage should be honored by all, and the marriage bed kept pure, for God will judge the adulterer and all the sexually immoral" (Hebrews 13:4, New International Version).

"Blessed is the man who endures temptation; for when he has been approved, he will receive the crown of life which the Lord has promised to those who love Him" (James 1:12).

"But each one is tempted when he is drawn away by his own desires and enticed. Then, when desire has conceived, it gives birth to sin; and sin, when it is full-grown, brings forth death. Do not be deceived, my beloved brethren" (James 1:14-16).

LOOKING INTO THE MIRROR

Romans 13:14 says, ". . . make no provision for the flesh, to fulfill the lusts thereof."

- What in the world does that mean?

- In what ways might you be making provision for your flesh, in order to fulfill its lust?

When Jesus stepped on the scene, His teaching concerning sexual immorality was much stricter than what His audience adhered to. He said things like, "You've heard it said, 'Don't commit adultery,' but I say to you, 'Whoever looks at a woman to lust after her has already committed adultery in his heart'" (Matthew 5: 27–28). But consider this—when dealing with this topic, no one shared a stronger message than Jesus; however, people who were guilty of the very thing He preached, wanted to be around Him.

- What does that say about Jesus?

Read John 8:1–12 then answer the following questions:

- Is there a difference between the way Jesus feels about sin and the way He feels about you? Please explain your answer.

- How do you think Jesus responds to us when we come to Him with our sin?

- What would you tell someone who has crossed sexual lines and drifted off into forbidden areas?

Friends . . . Who Needs 'Em?

In the chaos of teenage living, everyone needs a friend. Unfortunately, two things are often confused—friendship and popularity. The true friend is not always the most popular kid at school, and the most popular kid at school is not always the true friend. Someone once said, "If Barbie is so popular, why do you have to buy her friends?"

James 5:16 is a verse we should all use to measure true friendship. The verse says, "Confess your sins to one another, and pray for one another, that you may be healed. The effective, fervent prayer of a righteous man avails much." In this verse, we discover three things about genuine friendship:

1. Authentic friendship is a relationship built on trust.
2. A true friend takes my faults to God and to God alone.
3. Where confessions can be made, healing can take place.

According to James, if my friends cannot trust me with their secret sins and hidden habits, then I am keeping them from encountering the healing power of God. My friend should see me as trustworthy, loyal, supportive, and loving. If he doesn't see me that way, he will not confide in me. James says that it is through the prayers of this confident companionship that we experience healing. For years I've said, "God, I want to see the power of your Spirit move in my life!" The truth is, where there's a lack of true companionship, there's also a lack of power. For those of us who passionately wish to be used by God, James 5:16 is the measuring stick for how much God will use us. If we cannot be trusted with someone's confession, we cannot be used by God.

Some folks call these James 5:16 friends, "Accountability Partners." These are those who know you best, yet love you the most, those who listen well and pray hard, those who point out your faults without rubbing them in. Friends like these are a must-have for healthy Christian living.

Remember Noah, the guy who built the ark? In the book of Genesis, after the flood, Noah planted a vineyard. He drank from the vineyard, got a killer buzz, passed out, and lost his robe as he hit the floor. One of Noah's three sons walked in and saw his father lying there, naked and lit up. What did his son do? He found his two brothers and said, "You have got to come take a look at our old man!"

Now first of all, what kind of fellow gets a kick out of seeing his dad naked? I thought that was every kid's worst fear. And if that wasn't enough, he wanted to expose his dad's shame to the other sons as well. The two brothers refused to let curiosity get the best of them. They took a blanket, walked backward into their father's tent, dropped the cover, and left. Instead of being critical, they became a cover. Remember, dogs are man's best friends because they wag their tails and not their tongues. One of Noah's sons was cursed, and the other two were blessed. I'll let you guess which one was cursed.

First John 2:1 says, "My little children, these things I write to you, so that you may not sin. And if anyone sins, we have an Advocate with the Father, Jesus Christ the righteous." In this verse, the word advocate means, "to cover." Just like Noah's two sons covered his shame, Jesus has become our covering. He does not expose our shame; he covers our shame. The Bible calls Jesus a friend that sticks closer than a brother.

If you want to make friends and keep friends, be a James 5:16 person. Be someone whom others can come to in confidence. Be someone who challenges people without crushing them. Ask yourself this question: "If I were someone else, would I be friends with me?" I'll leave you with some of my favorite quotes on friendship:

- Deal with the faults of others as gently as you would your own.
- You can't eat your friends and have them too.
- Friendship is responsibility, not just an opportunity.
- Always hold your head up but be careful to keep your nose at a friendly level.
- Anyone can give advice, but a real friend will lend a helping hand.

LOOKING INTO THE MIRROR

People are multidimensional; you could say that people have more than one face! Even God is portrayed as having four faces (Revelation 4:7). However, all of God's faces are good!

- How do you respond when one of your friends shows another face?

Suicide

When all my hope is lost,
does that make me lost too?
When I feel empty and cold,
will Your hand be there for me to hold?

I feel like I'm slipping away,
and I don't have the strength to call on Your name.
But I know that with Your love,
I can make it throughout today.

By Tori Creech

A Journey Toward Suicide

Let's look at two characters in the Bible who committed suicide:

1. King Saul of the Old Testament
2. Judas of the New Testament

Saul was chosen to serve as the first king of Israel. He wasn't voted into office. He didn't lead a promising campaign. He was discovered by God and anointed by Samuel the prophet. Israel wanted a king and God found Saul worthy of the call.

During the early days of Saul's reign, his heart was humble. He clearly desired to please the Lord. The prophet said in 1 Samuel 15:17, "When you were little in your own eyes, were you not head of the tribes of Israel? And did not the Lord anoint you king over Israel?" But something slowly started changing in Saul's heart, and he became bitter and envious. Like so many other insecure leaders, he became jealous and paranoid. Over the years his heart hardened. He began listening to the people's requests more than he did to God's. Instead of seeking the prophet's advice, he consulted witches. In the end, his kingdom went to war and his army suffered a major defeat. The Bible says that King Saul fell on his own sword and took his life.

Judas was another man chosen by God. After spending forty days fasting and a night in prayer, Jesus chose His twelve disciples. Judas made the team. For three and a half years, Judas walked with Jesus. He, and the other disciples who were sent, healed the sick, cleansed lepers, raised the dead, cast out demons, and preached the Word of God. Judas also served as the treasurer, caring for the finances of the ministry.

But, just like Saul, something changed in Judas. The first sign of trouble is found in Matthew 26 and John 12. A woman began to radically worship at the feet of Jesus and Judas got ticked off about it. The seed of betrayal started to grow, and he buddied up with the enemy. Jesus was arrested, beaten, and killed for thirty pieces of silver. Judas had done the unthinkable. Guilt set in and Judas ended it all. He hanged himself from a tree in a nearby field.

In both of these cases, one thing is obvious: each one's journey toward suicide was a journey away from God. The closer they got to the end, the darker their lives became. Like kudzu vine, the weeds of bitterness choked out the fruit of the Spirit, and the end result was death.

LOOKING INTO THE MIRROR

- Bitterness is a deadly potion. Synonyms for bitterness are anguish, distress, harshness, hostility, pain, and sarcasm. What might be some other words associated with bitterness?

- Are there areas in your life in which you are bitter? If so, identify those things by writing them in the area below.

Failing Faith

While I was in high school, my family lost a dear loved one to suicide. Mom stayed with my aunt the night before she took her life. Mom said that she got up several times to check on her during the night. On several occasions, she thought she heard her crying. Brenda, my aunt, told Mom she only had a sinus cold and there was nothing to worry about. A few days later she was found dead several miles from her home.

I've often thought about a Bible verse that says, "Without faith it is impossible to please God" (Hebrews 11:6). Suicide is the absence of faith. A suicidal person is basically saying, "I've gone too far, this situation is too bad, and there is absolutely no way God can help me now." Suicide is the perfect example of someone who fails to trust God.

One day as I was driving to the post office, a car whipped in behind me and nearly took out my rear bumper. The driver started laying on the horn. The guy turned out to be a friend of mine in major distress. As soon as I hopped in the vehicle, he started crying like a young child. At the time, nothing was going well for him and every area of his life was under major attack. As he vented his frustration, I asked him if he had told God how aggravated he was. He looked at me like I had lost my mind. He said, "But I'm ticked off! And frankly I've got some issues with God right now." "Then tell Him that," I said. You see, I'm convinced that if God knows how we feel, He would rather us be honest with Him than to ignore Him.

First Peter 5:7 says that we should, "Cast your cares upon Jesus for He cares for you." The phrase "cast your cares" implies frustration, disgust, and outrage. We're better at presenting our cares than casting our cares. We update God with every detail, as if He's not checked His voicemail in a while. God wants to hear the bitter groan of our hearts as we release the burdens of our souls. But the important thing is where we release those burdens. Do we leave them in a bar, in a suicidal attempt, in the backseat of a car, or in the arms of Jesus? Someone once said, "You can tell a lot about a man by what he reaches for on his way down."

Psalm 46:1 says, "He is a present help in the time of trouble." If life brought you to it, God can bring you through it. Trust Him! Talk to Him! Cry out to Him! Don't just tell God how big your problem is; start telling your problems how big your God is.

Here are some practical tips during seasons of despair:

- Surround yourself with godly friends who can hold you accountable.
- Turn off the sad movies and sad songs, and put up the chocolates.
- Commit the promises of God to memory. Fill your house with sticky notes reminding you of God's faithfulness.

LOOKING INTO THE MIRROR

Everyone needs an emotional vocabulary. Look up the word happy in a thesaurus and you will find about eighty words; for the word sad, there are even more. You may find that you are not sad. Rather, you may be bitter, grief stricken, or heartbroken. Get to the root of your emotions.

- What emotion are you experiencing at this time in your life? Use a thesaurus to find the word that best expresses your feelings.

Heaven or Hell?

A young friend of mine came by the house one evening after hearing that one of his old friends had ended his life. As he sat there on my sofa crying with his face planted in his hands, he said, "What hurts me the most is, I know he's in hell." His friend had swallowed a handful of pills and was found dead a few hours later. Although I have a strong opinion about the eternal position of those who commit suicide, I questioned my friend's conclusion in this situation. I told him that in this case, we had no idea what took place after he ingested those pills. Maybe he called for help, he could have cried out to God. All I know is that I wouldn't want to stand before God in his shoes, but to say for certain that he is in hell, in this particular situation, I sure couldn't say that.

Let us not forget the Word of God says that when Christ appears, we should run out to meet Him with confidence. Whether He comes to meet us or we go to meet Him, confidence should fill our hearts and sadly, suicide replaces our confidence with many uncertainties. Hebrews 10:31 says, "It is a fearful thing to fall into the hands of a just and living God." The bottom line is, I wouldn't want to appear before God with a question mark in my heart.

We must also consider the leading causes of suicidal attempts. Suicide is often the result of bitterness toward a parent or parents. In that case, one sees suicide as the ultimate act of revenge. The son or daughter says, "The guilt of my death will cause my parents grief for the rest of their lives." Perhaps that bitterness is aimed toward a boyfriend or girlfriend who has done you wrong. Either way, bitterness is a primary cause of suicide. Hebrews 12:14–15 says, "Pursue peace with all people, and holiness, without which no one will see the Lord: looking carefully lest anyone fall short of the grace of God; lest any root of bitterness springing up cause trouble, and by this many become defiled."

With these things in mind, suicide must be viewed as a sinful act because it is born out of revenge, rejection, anger, selfishness, misery, and a lack of faith. These things are not found in the Bible's list of spiritual fruits.

Suicide is not the end of the problem; it's the beginning of a nightmare.

LOOKING INTO THE MIRROR

Have you ever lost someone close to you by suicide? You may find it helpful to write about the passing of your loved one.

- Try to journal your thoughts and feelings concerning the situation.

The Pride of Suicide

Failure is a common reason for suicide. When a secret moral failure is exposed, the weight of embarrassment becomes too heavy and the individual sees suicide as a means of escape. Over the years, we've seen this attempt among people who suffered a major business failure.

Several years ago, I launched a business that went belly up. I had borrowed money from a supportive family member and when I closed shop, the feeling of defeat hit me like a tidal wave. During that time, I had a hefty life insurance policy. I hate to admit it, but I often thought of (and dreamed of) paying back my family by ending my life. Think about what 2 Corinthians 7:10 says: "For godly sorrow works repentance to salvation . . . but the sorrow of the world works death." All of us experience times of sorrow, but godly sorrow turns us toward God. However, worldly sorrow ends in hopelessness and death.

Pride must also be addressed when investigating reasons for suicide. If a lady fails and suicide becomes her way of avoiding the embarrassment, she is actually saying, "I'm too proud to face my mistakes." Friends, "Pride comes before a fall." Scripture plainly says, "God resists the proud, but He gives grace to the humble." Pride was the single sin that transformed Lucifer from angel to devil.

Let us not forget that God is bigger than our failures. As a matter of fact, you won't even find the word failure in the Bible.

In scripture, there were two disciples who betrayed Jesus. We know that Judas had Jesus arrested, but Peter denied knowing Him. Both men failed. But godly sorrow brought one to salvation, while worldly sorrow brought the other to suicide. One man swallowed his pride; the other man hung from his.

If you've failed, it's not the end of the world. I'm not saying things will be better when you wake up tomorrow, but I do know that God has a reputation of turning our messes into masterpieces. Great people learn to overcome great failures. After years of failed attempts to create the light bulb, Thomas Edison said, "I have not failed. I've only learned 1,000 ways not to create the light bulb."

While struggling through my business loss, I made myself a list of Bible verses and declarations. Each morning as I started my day, I spoke those words over my life. I've listed a few of them below:

VERSES FOR LIFE'S ADVERSITIES

"I can do all things through Christ who gives me strength" (Philippians 4:13).

"I will not lack, because my God shall supply all of my needs according to His riches in glory" (Philippians 4:19).

"I shall not fear because God has not given me a spirit of fear, but of power, love, and a peaceful mind" (2 Timothy 1:7).

"I will not be weak; God's word says that the Lord is my strength" (Psalm 27:1).

"I will not allow Satan to rule over my life because God's word declares, 'Greater is He that is in me, than he that is in the world'" (1 John 4:4).

"I have no one to fear, knowing if God is for me, who can be against me?" (Romans 8:31).

"I am not alone in this battle. The word of God tells me that Jesus will never leave me nor will He forsake me" (Matthew 28:20 and Hebrews 13:5).

"The Spirit of the Lord gives me liberty; therefore, I shall not live in bondage" (Galatians 5:1).

"I will not worry or fret; I cast all my cares and anxieties on Christ who cares for me" (1 Peter 5:7).

"I will not be depressed. I will recall God's loving kindness, compassion, and faithfulness and I will have hope" (Lamentations 3:21–23).

"I am not hopelessly condemned. I am in Christ, and I will not walk in hopelessness or condemnation from failures. But I will walk in the joy of the Lord" (Romans 8:1–2).

"I am full of God's wisdom. He promised to grant me His wisdom every time I ask" (James 1:5).

"I will not feel like a failure because I am more than a conqueror in all things through Christ Jesus my Lord" (Romans 8:37).

"I shall not accept defeat. The Bible says that God will always lead me into triumph" (2 Corinthians 2:14).

"I shall not live in sickness or frailty, because the word of God tells me that it was by His stripes that I was healed" (Isaiah 53:5).

God's word over me is, "I'm blessed in the city, blessed in the country, blessed shall be the fruit of my body (my children) . . . The Lord will cause my enemies who rise up against me to be defeated before my face; they will come at me one way but run from me in seven different directions. The Lord will open to me His good treasures, the heavens, to give the rain to my land in its seasons, and to bless all the work of my hands. I will be a lender, but not a borrower. The Lord has made me the head and not the tail." (Deuteronomy 28:3–13).

LOOKING INTO THE MIRROR

- There's an old statement that goes like this: "Embarrassment is pride turned inside out." Do you agree with this statement? Take a few minutes and support your answer.

Make Pain Your Platform

Dave Pelzar was born in 1960 and grew up in a middle-class suburb of San Francisco. His mother was a homemaker and an alcoholic who started abusing him when he was four years old. While his mother cared for the rest of the family, Dave was starved, locked in a closet, beaten, often burned, and was referred to as "It."

His mother made him daily eat his brother's waste. She daily made him drink ammonia, swallow soap, and sip on bleach. Believe it or not, no one stopped the mother! Teachers noticed David's strange behavior, but nothing was done until 1972. For eight years, he lived through this nightmare.

From age twelve to eighteen, Dave lived in a series of foster homes. Fearing that he would be homeless once he became too old for foster care living, he dropped out of school and worked double shifts at a local factory. He later earned his GED and joined the air force.

What do you think happened to Dave? In light of his abuse and daily torment, where do you think Dave is now? Dave has won many awards and commendations from presidents such as: Ronald Reagan, both President Bush and George W. Bush, and President Bill Clinton. In 1993, Dave was honored as one of the ten most outstanding Americans, and in 1994, his effort in child-abuse prevention earned him the distinction as one of the only U.S. citizens to be nominated as an Outstanding Person of the World.

Dave is a highly sought-after speaker and has authored the following books: *The Lost Boy, A Man Name Dave, A Child Called It, The Privilege of Youth, Help Yourself,* and *Help Yourself For Teens.*

I heard Dave's story several years ago. When I heard of his sorrow and his success, it became obvious to me that somehow Dave managed to make his pain his platform. He used his adversity to his advantage.

I have found that in times of intense disappointments, some people grow wings while others buy crutches. The tougher it gets, the higher some soar, while others limp around bitter and wounded, always blaming others for their misery. Someone once said, "Pain is unavoidable, but misery is optional."

One of my favorite Bible characters is Joseph. He was a young man with a dream. He wanted his life to count for something. I can relate to someone like that.

However, several things went wrong, and Joseph's story became one tragedy after another. His jealous brothers betrayed him, threw him into a pit, and sold him into slavery. Years later, he was falsely accused and thrown into prison. Decades later, his story began to change. He found favor with Pharaoh, the king of Egypt. He rose to power and became second in command of Pharaoh's kingdom. A famine struck Joseph's homeland. His brothers heard there was food in Egypt. As fate would have it, they found themselves at Joseph's feet, begging for food and forgiveness. Joseph gave them both. His words were, "What you meant for evil, God meant for good." What a great example of using your adversity to your advantage. We must always look for purpose in the pain. What is God up to? Sometimes a breakdown will lead us to a breakthrough.

LOOKING INTO THE MIRROR

- Think about an area of pain. Imagine ways that God could use that painful experience—list a few.

- List a good Bible story that illustrates one of the ways that you've mentioned.

What about Samson?

One Sunday evening a young girl in our church asked me if Samson went to hell for committing suicide. I said, "Samson did not commit suicide." Throughout Samson's life he had fought many battles against the Philistines. The Philistines were constantly terrorizing Israel, attacking them whenever the opportunity arose. God used Samson to defend His people from the hand of the Philistines. In one battle, Samson single-handedly killed 1,000 Philistines with the jaw bone of an ass.

This is totally off the subject, but I'm a big *Sanford and Son* fan. I remember Fred Sanford telling Aunt Esther that Samson killed a thousand Philistines with her jaw bone. Man that's funny!

Okay, back to the point. Samson wandered away from the Lord. His desire for wild living outweighed his desire for the things of God. As a result, his lady sold him out and the Philistines had their man. One day the Philistines gathered at the temple built for the Philistine god, Dagon. Samson was led into the temple and was chained between two pillars. While thousands watched, Samson prayed the same prayer that the thief on the cross prayed: "Remember me." With all his might, he pushed, the pillars broke, the temple collapsed, the Philistines were killed, and Samson died beneath the rubble.

Now, did Samson kill himself? No! He was not attempting suicide; he was fighting for his country. He believed freedom was worth dying for. I asked the young lady at church, "If someone tried to shoot you and your daddy jumped in front of you, knowing that by doing so he would probably die, would you call that suicide?" Of course she said, "No." Samson did the same thing. He died defending his people.

We also find Samson listed among the heroes of faith. Hebrews, chapter eleven, lists a group of people who were used by God in incredible ways. Everyone listed faced extreme hardship and disappointments, but none of them gave in. Samson is one of those names mentioned in the chapter. If Samson committed suicide, why is his name found among those who refused to quit when times got tough?

LOOKING INTO THE MIRROR

When you sacrifice something, you lose all control of what's being offered. Suicide is not an act of giving but an act of taking—the taking of one's life.

- How are sacrifice and suicide different?

Better Safe than Sorry

Melissa has been a registered nurse since before we were married. She's worked in about every nursing environment imaginable. Her experience ranges from health departments, community hospitals, one of America's largest hospitals, and nursing homes. She's taught nursing on a university level, and she's wiped the noses of our two precious children, Tori and Chaz.

Melissa has treated her fair share of suicide attempts. She is currently carpooling with Angie, who's been a friend of ours for several years now. This morning I picked her up at Angie's house and we started back home. It's about a twenty-minute drive and normally she would have conked out but not this morning. Through the night she had cared for a lady who almost succeeded in an attempt to take her life. Of course, I don't know all the details. What she was able to share with me was heartbreaking.

The lady had been battling a serious case of depression for some time. She sent a text message to her sister and said she wanted to close her eyes and go to sleep. A little later, she sent another text, but it didn't make any sense. She had taken a hand full of pills and the deadly dose had begun to take effect. As you can imagine, the family was terrified. They began searching and she was found lying unconscious on her mother's grave. The suicide note in her hand said: "I just want my mommy to hold me again."

In most cases, someone shows a series of warning signs before they end it all. Some warnings may include deathly fascinations, morbid music, cutting, satanic or disturbing doodles, or in this case, her desire to "close her eyes and sleep" was the sign of a problem. Many victims will show obvious signs of depression: a drop in grades, lack of energy, low ambition, and little concern for his or her appearance. Others may express outbursts of anger and irritability.

Regardless of the signs, if someone remotely hints of hurting his or her self, tell someone. Don't tell a group of people. Tell a trustworthy adult. Go to your school guidance counselor or principal. If that's not an option, tell a parent. Remember, it's better to be safe than sorry. After my aunt's death, my mom repeatedly said, "If I had only said this or done that." If you have a gut feeling that someone you love is suicidal, talk to him or her. Go with your gut instinct. If nothing else, let them know how much they mean to you and how willing you are to lend them an ear.

Studies reveal that 10 percent of those who make a first attempt will eventually take their own lives.

LOOKING INTO THE MIRROR

- Would you say that suicide is an act of control? Why or why not?

- What are some consequences of suicide?

- What might you say to someone who displays suicidal tendencies?

Before You Go

Thanks so much for taking this journey with me. Hopefully you've found some insight along the way. Life can be a mess from time to time. Quite often I've picked up a book at just the right time. It was like the author knew what I needed to hear. I trust this book found its way to you at the perfect moment. Before you go, can I pray a prayer over you? I knew you wouldn't mind. Here it goes . . .

"Lord Jesus, thank You for my new friends. I'm asking You to reveal Yourself to them in an incredible way. More than ever before, open the windows of heaven upon them. Surprise them with gifts that leave them speechless—mouth and eyes wide open in amazement. Dazzle them with Your love. Overcome them with a fresh outpouring of Your Spirit. Do the things I don't know to ask for. Reveal to them what You see in them and what You wish they saw in You. Give them a new zeal for Your presence and Your word. Help them to forget about the things that no longer matter. Thank You, Lord Jesus." Amen.

Thanks again.

Until next time,
Jason Creech

Endnotes

[1] Lee Strobel, *The Case for a Creator Student Edition* (Zondervan, Grand Rapids, Michigan 49530) pp. 74–75.

[2] Lee Strobel, *The Case for a Creator Student Edition* (Zondervan, Grand Rapids, Michigan 49530) p. 69.

[3] Noel Botham, *The Best Book of Useless Information Ever* (Penguin Group London, England) p. 96.

[4] Phil Callaway, *Who Put My Life on Fast-Forward?* (Harvest House Publishers, Eugene, Oregon 97404) p. 10.

[5] Craig Gross & Mike Foster, *Questions You can't ask your Mama About Sex* (Zondervan, Grand Rapids, Michigan 49530) pp. 43–44.

TO LEARN MORE ABOUT MIRROR-MIRROR VISIT US ONLINE AT

ONEMIRROR.NET

Publishing

Check out these additional titles by author Jason Creech.

These books will be available Summer 2011 in paperback, Amazon Kindle™, Apple iPad™, and Barnes & Noble Nook™ editions.

New.U by Jason Creech
Are you just getting started as a new Christian? Then you probably have a lot of questions. In this four-week devotional, you'll discover a boat-load of answers. Learn the simplicity of the Christian life. Welcome to freedom. Welcome to the new u.

Navigate by Jason Creech
For most of our Christian journey we search for God's will. But what if we have it all wrong? What if we don't have to search for God's will? What if God's will searches for us?

Introducing *Blinders* by Kristy Shelton…

Blinders, a novel by Kristy Shelton, portrays a beautiful relationship between a former slave couple, their love for a boy who wanders onto their farm, and the redeeming forgiveness of the heavenly Father. In this inspirational novel, Eugene, an eleven-year-old boy growing up in Kentucky in 1912, is drawn to a light in the distance that compels him to run away from his abusive stepfather. He is led to the farm of Franklin and Rachel Hawkins who live in a rundown house built on top of a cave yet have magnificent thoroughbred horses grazing in their bluegrass pasture. Eugene is adopted into the family, and as he grows up, gradually discovers secrets from the past that keep Franklin and Rachel isolated on their remote farm. Eugene is severely tested when he is seized from the farm at the age of sixteen and forced into the Great War now raging in France. He embarks on a dangerous journey that will put his life and faith to the test. When he returns two years later as a man, his only hope is to give his incredible burden of guilt to the One who can save him, and allow a mother's unconditional love to help him fulfill his destiny. Available Spring 2011 in hardback, paperback, Amazon Kindle™, and Apple iPad™ editions.

ABOUT INNOVO PUBLISHING LLC

Innovo Publishing LLC is a full-service Christian publishing company serving the Christian and wholesome markets. Innovo creates, distributes, and markets quality books, eBooks, audiobooks, music, and videos through traditional and innovative publishing models and services. Innovo provides distribution, marketing, and automated order fulfillment through a network of thousands of physical and online wholesalers, retailers, bookstores, music stores, schools, and libraries worldwide. Innovo provides a unique combination of traditional publishing, co-publishing, and independent (self) publishing arrangements that allow authors, artists, and organizations to accomplish their personal, organizational, and philanthropic publishing goals. Visit Innovo Publishing's web site at www.innovopublishing.com or email Innovo at info@innovopublishing.com.

www.ingramcontent.com/pod-product-compliance
Lightning Source LLC
Chambersburg PA
CBHW021015090426
42738CB00007B/796